LINE SHOOT

VANWELL
VOICES
of WAR

ARTHUR SAGER

LINE SHOOT

DIARY OF A FIGHTER PILOT

Vanwell
PUBLISHING LIMITED

St. Catharines, Ontario

Vanwell Publishing acknowledges the financial support of the Government of
Canada through the Book Publishing Industry Development Program for our publishing activities.

Design: Linda Moroz-Irvine
Cover: Art Sager in Spit 5A, 1942. Below, members of 443 Squadron RCAF.

Vanwell Publishing Limited
1 Northrup Crescent
P.O. Box 2131
St. Catharines, Ontario L2R 7S2

Printed in Canada

National Library of Canada Cataloguing in Publication

Sager, Arthur, 1916-
          Line shoot : diary of a fighter pilot / Arthur Sager.

(Vanwell voices of war)

ISBN 1-55125-059-4
ISSN 1498-8844

    1. Sager, Arthur, 1916- 2. World War, 1939-1945—Aerial operations, Canadian.
3. Canada. Royal Canadian Air Force—Biography. 4. Fighter pilots—Biography.
I. Title. II. Series.

D811.D3223 2002   940.54'4971'092   C2002-903861-8

CONTENTS

PREFACE

I was working in England as an actor when war was declared on September 3rd, 1939. In the preceding months I had been compelled to think about what I would do if war came. In London that summer my friend from the *Daily Mirror*, Cecil Ashwell, told me that he had received his conscription papers. He admitted that had he not been conscripted he would have volunteered. "We've no choice," he said. "We lost the chance to stop Hitler and the only way to stop him now is to fight." He'd been a firm pacifist like me and this renunciation of his convictions made me wonder about my own.

Soon after, I found myself writing a newspaper article about a refugee camp for Jews from Germany and Austria. Interviewing the pitiful refugees brought home to me the inhumanity of Hitler's racial policies and in a vivid way the reasons for Cecil's volte-face. By August I knew that if war came I would be a fighter pilot, high in the air where you fought one to one!

Unable to get into the RAF, I returned to Canada in December to join the RCAF. After paying off travel debts I applied for aircrew training in October 1940 and was called up in February 1941. Throughout the following four and a half years I kept a full diary. As, surprisingly, there remains some interest in our derring-do of sixty years ago, I have brought these diary notes together and present them in the hope they will be accepted as being within forgivable bounds of line shooting.

Dedicated to Phil 'P.G.' Blades, fellow flight commander and closest friend, who nitpicked the first draft but still urged me to get on with it. In Heaven now, he'll be probing the book for split infinitives and double negatives. Cheers, chum!

CHAPTER I

Learning To Be a Fighter Pilot

On February 28th, 1941 I boarded a train in Vancouver, bound for the manning pool in Brandon, Manitoba. Finally I was in the Air Force, on the way to becoming a fighter pilot—or at least I hoped so. I felt liberated, and the feelings of guilt were almost gone about not having joined up in England a year and a half before.

There were fourteen others on the draft, some in their teens, and at twenty-four I felt like an old man. Not for long, however, as when we got talking and joking over smuggled beer I lost the sense of seniority and happily became an ageless member of the group. While the day's papers carried stories of the bombing of English cities no one talked about the war. It was as if we were on safari.

We were dressed casually and carried small bags with pyjamas, change of underwear and toilet articles. "Wear warm but disposable clothing as uniforms will be issued in Brandon," the instructions had said. As it was still winter some of us had jackets and I felt sorry for the two recruits from California dressed for a beach in Malibu.

The pleasant sensation of anonymity, of comradeship without identity, was strengthened when we arrived at Brandon where we were lined up on the platform by a burly corporal and marched out of step to the sprawling barracks that looked like a prison. It was bitterly cold: fingers, nose and ears froze en route and the two Californians were blue on arrival. We marched first to a drill hall to thaw out and then to a long hut with double-decker bunks. "Put your stuff on any one and get back on the double to the drill hall," the corporal shouted. This we did meekly, and thus began our introduction to military life, to the subjugation of personality and the transformation of individuals into obedient sheep.

It was our introduction as well to the most wearisome activity of training—waiting. You waited for everything: for winter underwear and uniforms, toilet articles and towel, sheets and blankets; to see the doctor, dentist, tailor and, if you wanted, the padre; to sign papers, make a will, be X-rayed, get fingerprinted; to eat, attend lectures, get paid. I waited a week for a wedge cap that didn't fall off and boots that didn't produce blisters.

You couldn't be bashful in the Air Force. We stripped, stood naked in line, walked past the M.O. who looked into your mouth and up your bottom, past corporals who stuck a needle into your left arm going down and scratched your right arm going back, and later you stripped again to have your working parts examined in a primly-called "short arm inspection."

We were lectured to: by the doctor on venereal disease and informed on the use of the "French letter;" by the Adjutant on Air Force regulations; by a sergeant-major on saluting—how, where and when not to do it. And every day, morning and afternoon, we were shouted at by corporals and sergeants and drilled in military evolutions, all the while being reminded in colourful adjectives of our hopeless incompetence. We were intimidated by the awesome Warrant Officer, king of the drill hall, six and a half feet of magnificently structured manhood in a uniform chiselled to his frame, with a moustache bristling with electricity and a voice that threatened the eardrums.

Mutinous thoughts entered my head about the relevance for a would-be fighter pilot of this daily drilling. Perhaps it was the quickest way to convert a civilian into a cipher, into an airman who kept in formation, at least on the ground. In any case I came to accept, and at times even to enjoy, this marching in unison and the discipline of it. And there were feelings of physical well-being on long route marches, keeping in step to the corporal's "Left, Right!" and to songs, shouted rather than sung, and returning to barracks tired, mindless and hungry.

There were endless chores at a manning pool and the Air Force had devised subtle ways of securing manpower for them. On a roll call in the first week some of us innocently responded to the corporal's appeal for volunteers "for a special assignment" and we ended up in the kitchen washing windows and floors. Those late for P.T. were despatched to clean toilets while those who skipped it and were caught were confined to barracks and assigned to daily garbage collection. Untidy members of the Flight whose sheets didn't line up exactly or whose socks were found under the bed swept floors and raked the yard. Pack drill was reserved for more serious offenders, and only when Flights had achieved their quota of sinners for normal work assignments.

To relieve the monotony films were shown occasionally in the evenings. These were always packed. But few attended the voluntary lectures on current affairs and even fewer bought newspapers on sale in the mess. Men who volunteered for war seemed to avoid talking or reading about it. The favourite topic was women and on this subject interesting—and to me novel—aspects were exposed after lights out. Despite the over-abundance of uniformed males in Brandon girls were easy to pick up, if you could believe the boasting of those who tried it. Mind fixed on becoming a pilot and content with male comradeship, at least at that stage, I limited myself to one church-sponsored Saturday night dance followed by a walk in a park on Sunday with the shy girl who had courageously agreed to venture onto the dance floor with me.

As the weeks went by time began to drag. Drafts were called and disappeared, newcomers arrived. We began to feel like veterans, the smartest on the drill floor, the most rebellious elsewhere. We read every bulletin, listened to every broadcast announcement, devoured every rumour. My name appeared on a draft list twice but the movement was twice postponed. Finally the real one came through and, typically, we were given only a few hours' notice. We rushed to pack, return property assigned to us, sign papers, get marching orders and we were hustled onto a train for Winnipeg, there to do guard duty at a supply depot.

If the six weeks at manning pool had a disciplinary purpose, the four on guard duty had none save to inculcate patience.

What need to mount guard on a well-fenced depot in peaceful Winnipeg, to patrol the perimeter with bullet-free rifles on freezing nights when even delinquents were cuddled in bed? The corporals warned darkly of fifth column enemies outside the stockade but we knew their stories were a ruse. When we accepted them as such and when we recognized that the depot was merely a holding point in the clogged-up training queue we relaxed, at least for the first two weeks. There was little drilling, no parades and no route marches, and the corporals were human. And we did learn how to dismantle an Enfield.

It was April but still winter in Winnipeg and at the corner of Portage and Main, where we went to gawk at the prettiest girls in Canada, who worked at Eatons, we took refuge from the Arctic gale in bus stops and shop doorways. But while their climate was frigid, the hearts of Winnipeggers were warm. Two steps along the street into town you were picked up, driven to your destination even if it was out of the way and often taken to dinner. But I had little need to rely on the spontaneous hospitality of prairie folk. I was the envy of the station as on every twenty-four-hour pass I was claimed at the main gate by a beautiful girl in a huge Buick. She was Betty Thomas, daughter of friends of the family who opened their home and hearts to the homesick airman. Lapping up the glory of having so handsomely "scored," I refrained from divulging the family connection.

It was May 17th and summer when we reported to No. 2 Initial Training School in Regina. ITS was a ground training centre for would-be aircrew and here matters became serious. At the end of the five-week course they marked your fateful onward movement form with "P" for Pilot or "O" for Observer. I'd shoot myself before becoming an Observer and I started plotting on how to avoid doing so.

About twenty of us were assigned to M Flight under Corporal Minshall. "Old Smiley" they called him. He had protruding teeth, a juicy voice, and he was a nice fellow. It was he who later gave me good advice about getting a "P" rating. "Don't get top marks in anything except Link," he said. The Link Trainer, a computer ahead of its time, was an enclosed, revolving box with instruments in which you learned the basics of flying.

There were seven subjects: Mathematics, Navigation, Wireless, Armaments, Law and Discipline, Sanitation and Hygiene and, for some strange reason, Woodcraft, plus from four to six hours on the Link. It was like going back to high school but everything was easier, including Mathematics which was taught by a nervously befuddled instructor. Navigation was new and interesting but the instructor was a Tartar. Wireless was new too, difficult at first but easy when you got the hang of it. Armaments was boring, taught by a dimwit, and in Law and Discipline a kindly old chap put everyone and almost himself to sleep.

Instinctively, I threw myself into study, avoiding free-for-alls in the barracks and beer sallies outside, sometimes swotting up in the reading room of the YMCA. For relaxation, ping-pong and coke, Brant Howell, my pal in M Flight, and I would go to the Hostess Club run by Mrs. McVicar and it was there we met Mary and Marj whom we later took boating on the lake. Apart from this outing and a dance in the Armouries where I watched more than waltzed I again stayed clear of the fair sex.

Classes, drill and P.T. filled all the on-duty hours. We were brought to life by a bugle at 6:45 a.m., made beds, shaved, washed, showered if there was time, polished shoes, shined buttons, breakfasted, and went to parade for the C/O's inspection at 8:15. Classes began at nine. I took my turn on Duty Watch and Fire Picket, never missed a roll call and never ran afoul of the corporals. I even practised extra drill voluntarily for the Lieutenant-Governor's Parade and a Wing Parade installing a new C/O. I was a model student. "Ease up!" Brant said. "You're getting a reputation as an apple polisher."

One evening at the Hostess Club we talked to four fellows in the senior squadron who had finished the course and were waiting for a draft. They had been assigned to Observer School and were happy about it. All were my age, two a bit older, and all had received good marks in Mathematics, Navigation and Law and Discipline, top character ratings in "Responsible Behaviour" but below average marks on the Link Trainer. It was after this encounter that Corporal Minshall warned me about becoming an egghead.

The Link Trainer was no problem as I enjoyed it, but just to make sure I asked and got extra sessions. I'd have to go easy in the exams perhaps but what about the character reference, the responsible behaviour bit? Brant, a one-track pilot like me, suggested a way to blot our copybook—go AWOL, Absent Without Leave. On the 36-hour pass before the exams we hitch-hiked to Qu'Appelle Valley where we swam, hiked, slept out of doors and deliberately returned to the station six hours late. We were confined to barracks, lost one day's pay and had AWOL marked on our records, which clearly implied a satisfactory degree of irresponsibility.

It was a bit difficult to weasel on the exams but I messed up one question in Mathematics, ignored another, fudged on Navigation and waffled about on Law and Discipline. Marks in all three were above average but not dangerously so and I got over 90 percent on the Link.

The final hurdle was the Personal Interview. I'd rehearsed carefully for this and, referring shamelessly to my egocentric pre-war career, argued that I was an individualist who'd make a hash of things as a crew member in a bomber. Though he said nothing, the interviewing officer clearly agreed. In any case he gave me the blessed "P."

We waited and waited for the draft, fingers crossed, soaking up every rumour. Finally the call came through. It was for Elementary Flying School in Vancouver. I got drunk on three beers that night.

I discovered the joy of flying on July 4th, one day after reporting to No. 8 EFTS on Sea Island. It was an unexpected and overwhelming experience. I was excited when I climbed into the Tiger Moth with McPherson, my first instructor, excited when the flimsy craft soared upwards and became a bird, more excited still when, my hands lightly on the stick as instructed, it climbed and dived and dipped like a feather in the wind. Looking down and about I sensed a freedom, a joyous freedom that made me sing; it was an intense, emotional release from earthbound ties. After landing and before getting out I asked McPherson if we could go up again but he smiled and shook his head. I left the kite dazed with delight.

R.S. Angus became my permanent instructor. He was quiet, calm, deliberate, even-tempered. After the second lesson I pleaded for more and longer flights and he obliged and then, bursting with self-confidence, I asked to go solo before the normal ten hours. Dubiously, he let me try on the 15th of July. "But just one circuit," he cautioned. Cocksure, half-drunk with excitement, I applied throttle and took off, sang around the circuit, came in too fast and too high and landed, or at least made approximate contact with the ground, in three huge bounces. Angus, grim-faced, waved me around again and this time, sober, I brought her in more smoothly, earning a thumbs up and a relieved smile.

But if flying solo was thrilling, aerobatics was doubly so. This came later in the course and when it did I couldn't get enough of it. I hurled the Moth about like a madman whenever I was up alone: power dives, loops, rolls off the top, barrel rolls, stall turns, inversions, spins. I liked cutting the motor at 8,000 feet and stalling, letting the kite plunge to earth out of control, round and round, down and down, waiting to the last moment to push the stick forward, gun the motor and pull out. And I'd side-slip in on landings, the wind blowing in from the side, until Angus warned against overdoing it. But he was lenient as he knew of my fighter pilot pretensions.

Tail chasing and formation flying were fun, instrument flying less so, and cross-countries, straight and level while map reading were boring—relatively speaking, as the adjective was inapplicable to any form of flight. Low flying at telephone pole level was pure joy and forced dead-stick landings an exciting challenge.

There was ground school as well at EFTS, five hours of classes in Navigation, Theory of Flight, Engines, Wireless, Link Trainer. We attended classes either in the morning or afternoon and flew during the other half of the day. Now that I was a pilot, or on the way to becoming one, I could relax and apply myself without worrying about high marks.

While No. 8 EFTS was an RCAF training centre it had grown out of a private flying school and was operated like one under a Station Manager. The discipline was not rigid and relations between students, teachers and flying instructors were friendly and informal. Finney, the Chief Ground School Instructor, and Milne, the Chief Flying Instructor, were respected for their ability, not their rank.

It was full summer in Vancouver and the days were long, sunny and warm. Between classes and while waiting to fly we played football and sunbathed, eyes cocked on those in the circuit and commenting expertly on every duff landing. There were two or three ground loops, one crash that wrote off the plane but not the pilot, and during our period on the course several students were "washed out" and grounded, disappearing into oblivion.

Apart from an occasional visit to the family in Burnaby, I avoided social activity, having no desire to re-establish contact with friends, all of whom were civilians leading separate lives. Compared with people in Brandon, Winnipeg and Regina, Vancouverites seemed unfriendly and uninterested in the war and no one picked you up when you waited for a bus into town. At one point however I relented and went to a dance at the Palomar with Bob McKeown, then a reporter on the *Sun*. He had a girlfriend and offered to get me a blind date. She was Dorothy Planche. We hit it off from the start and during the last two weeks in Vancouver had a number of enjoyable evenings together.

The momentous day came on the 11th of August when a visiting Air Force officer arrived to give the 50-hour flying test. It turned out to be anticlimactic as the officer was clearly bored, coming to life only when he thought I wasn't going to pull out on a spin. Angus said he'd given me an "above average" rating and my ego was further inflated when I got good marks in the exams, second-best on the Link. I was now a pilot and proud to be one.

But pride comes before a fall. A week later when I was posted for Service Training to Saskatoon my dreams of becoming a fighter pilot were shattered. No. 4 SFTS had twin-engine Cessna Cranes, not Harvards, and was obviously a training school for bomber pilots. Angry and losing a bit of control, I burst into Milne's office and demanded a change in posting. The CFI was at first thrown off by my mutinous behaviour but nice fellow that he was, he tried to calm me down. "I can't change the posting," he said. "But don't worry, some of the graduates from Saskatoon go on to fighters." I swore to myself that I'd be one of them!

As it turned out, apart from worrying about the outcome, I enjoyed the two months of service flying. The station was new, the barracks comfortable, the food good, there was little parading and no pack drill. Esprit de corps was excellent and, this being the last stage before getting one's Wings, the students were serious and keen, seldom returning to base at night under the weather. And, though it had two engines, the Cessna was a nice aircraft to fly.

Besides, I had a "home" in Saskatoon. On the first day off, waiting at the bus stop, I was picked up by a Mr. and Mrs. Stevens, taken on a drive around the city and invited to their place for dinner. They had a son who was at university and a pretty, nineteen-year-old daughter called Jay. With no objections on my part, the parents adopted me as a second son and on every pass thereafter I moved into the guest room of their spacious home in the suburbs, happily doffing uniform and becoming a civilian. We went to church together on Sundays, on drives into the country, and took Jay to movies and dances. She became my sister, and perhaps just a little bit more.

However, these regular periods of relaxation did not remove the inner fretting as No. 14 SFTS was clearly a school for bomber pilots. Emphasis was given to navigation on the ground and in the air, to meteorology, flying on instruments and night flying. Sometimes you went up as an Observer, getting queasy in the back seat while working out changes in course according to the wind and estimated ground speed. There were six navigation and three instrument flying tests and when they came I was relieved to get no more than "satisfactory" in any of them.

But I was lucky in my flying instructor. Sergeant Ruppel, an ex bush pilot in his mid-thirties, was a gruff man of few words, hard to get to know but likeable when you did. He was a frustrated fighter pilot who'd wanted to go overseas but was denied it because of his age. When I told him of my ambition he immediately became an ally.

After four hours dual he let me go solo and I pleased him as well as myself by coming in with only one bounce. The Cessna Crane was manoeuvrable and easy to land but you couldn't loop or spin it. It had a retractable undercarriage, adjustable flaps, gyroscopic instruments and other modern features but with its wooden main spar it didn't take kindly to rough treatment, unlike the Tiger Moth.

Sergeant Ruppel put me through the required regimen of cross-country navigation flights, instrument flying under the hood, formation flying, forced landings with one engine and without either of them. But he also taught me tricks not in the instruction manual. Far from the base, he'd show me how to do a semi-loop without straining the main spar and how to stall turn, slip, start into a spin and get out of it before losing control. He loved low flying, shaving the grass and edging over trees, and he was an expert in dead-stick landings. Cutting the engines without warning, he'd tell me quietly what to do: get into a safe glide, calculate the wind, pick a field, control the speed by slipping off, take her down to a few hundred feet, gun the motors and pull out. To make it real, he'd cut the motors in the circuit and tell me exactly where to put her down on the runway. One gained more confidence in the plane and in oneself from his unorthodox lessons than from any others.

We did a lot of solo cross-countries toward the end of the course—pre-planned navigation flights they were supposed to be—but if you got lost over the featureless prairie you could always find out where you were by dropping down and reading the name of the town on the railway station or grain elevator. I was often lost as I'd abandon the exercise to do gentle aerobatics and practice forced landings.

Night flying was a challenge as there was always a temptation to take your eyes off the instruments and rely on the stars and the lights below. The first time one student looked up he saw flames from the exhaust, thought he was on fire, and Control had to talk him out of using his parachute. I came to enjoy flying alone in the dark, the engines purring softly and the troublesome world out of sight.

In the ground school exams in mid-October I had reasonable marks, a good one on the Link, but I sensed that my future hinged on the Wings Test on the 21st. Desperate now about my rating, I suggested to Sergeant Ruppel that I might fly under the bridge in Saskatoon, as a previous student had done, to demonstrate a quality inconsistent with that of a responsible bomber pilot. He counselled strongly against it. "The fool who did it was grounded for good," he told me. "But stop worrying," he added with a grin.

The 21st came and I was assigned to F/L Millar for the fateful test. I was nervous, hurried on the cockpit check and hauled the plane into the air roughly. However, I began to relax at 10,000 feet when the officer asked for power dives, steep turns, stalls and other, for me, gentle manoeuvres. And when he cut the engines Sergeant Ruppel was beside me in spirit as I reported where I proposed to land and how. In the low flying area we went so low I could feel him tensing up and he was ready to take the stick when I brought the kite down without engines to the start of the runway.

As we were taxiing in the Flight Lieutenant said, "Sergeant Ruppel tells me you want to be a fighter pilot?"

"Yes, Sir!" I replied, trying not to shout. "That's why I joined the Air Force!"

He smiled, said nothing, but I found out later that he'd given me an "Average Plus" and recommended the precious S.E., Single-Engine rating. As far as I knew, I was the only one in the class to go on to fighters.

At the Wings Parade, all of us now Sergeant Pilots, we marched smartly up front in turn to have wings pinned on by the Commanding Officer. That night there was a banquet at which I drank beyond my limited capacity and Jay's brother, who had come to pick me up, kindly walked me around town to sober up before taking me home.

On November 9th I returned to Vancouver on embarkation leave. Dorothy and I were married on the 13th, she came with me to Halifax, and the boat left in the first week of December. The crossing was long, rough and boring, relieved only by rumours of submarines and poker over Drambuies in the bar. We officers were crammed into double-decker bunks but our cabins were spacious compared with the dungeons for sergeants below. We arrived in Liverpool on Christmas Day and on Boxing Day boarded a slow train for Bournemouth.

This seaside resort, known for its gentility, was chock-a-block with boisterous Canadian aircrew awaiting operational training and it was amazing that the natives were still friendly. Old people stopped you on the street to thank you for "coming over to help out." Some of us were lodged, two or more to a room, in the Metropole Hotel but we quickly savvied up and ate at the Anglo-Swiss where the food was better and the queues shorter. During the first two weeks we were documented for the umpteenth time, photo'd and issued identity cards, but apart from casual morning parades there was no program and we killed time by walking the waterfront, bussing into the country, sipping tea in the afternoon, quaffing beer in pubs at night, and dancing at the Pavillion. Like all towns in England, Bournemouth was blacked out from dusk to dawn but, as one wag said, "Even ugly girls are pretty in the dark."

The waiting palled, and in the third week I applied for a week's leave. First to dear old London, and there, in spite of the havoc wrought by air raids, disruption of everyday lives, short rations and all, the atmosphere was vibrant, almost cheerful, and the doughty Londoners were friendlier than ever.

The first calls were sad ones. At the *Daily Mirror* where I'd worked as a reporter there was confirmation that my pal, Cecil Ashwell, had been killed in France, and in Catford I couldn't find my friends, the Shearers, as their apartment and others in their area had been completely destroyed.

But I did find my cockney landlady in Stockwell. Mrs. 'ook, as bubbly as ever, hugged me warmly when I knocked on her door at 59 Kimberley Road and, chattering away, took me up to "my" room as though I'd been expected. When Mr. 'ook came home they ushered me down to the basement, their air raid shelter, to see the map of London on the wall with its coloured flags marking bomb explosions. They were proudest of the flags that were closest. They would be even prouder in 1944 when a buzz bomb removed the roof of their house and they had to move in with neighbours. But Mrs. 'ook never lost her cool. "We'll get rid of that 'orrible man 'itler," she said with absolute certainty. Her two regular boarders, her "gentlemen," were now in the Services but their rooms were kept ready for them when on leave in London. As was mine for the following three years.

After two nights at the Hooks I spent three with the Argyles at their cottage in Bridge near Canterbury. Dorrie Argyle, actress and once the love of my life, had married her cousin, now in the army, and was with him in Scotland. But her sister Betty and her father took time off from their voluntary war work and we went for long walks, played golf, and in the evenings visited the local pub, their community centre.

Back in London and first to B.C. House, my refuge when I was broke in 1938, and then to St. James's Court where I'd been a lift boy. Old Mrs. O'Hagan, one of the residents, greeted me. "Oh, the young Canadian!" she said, pulling me down to her level to make sure. The manager, Mr. Durrant, was still there and he insisted on giving me dinner in the restaurant where Mr. Hook, chief of the wine cellar, kept my glass full with the best claret. In a pleasant glow I felt my way in the blackout to Victoria Station to catch the last train for Bournemouth.

There, things had changed. Alert to the danger, alcoholic and other, of inactivity, the administration had introduced a program of morning and afternoon lectures. These were supposed to be voluntary but a degree of persuasion was added by the appointment of squad commanders responsible for ensuring attendance. I had the dubious honour of being made one of them but never succeeded in rounding up more than half of my twenty reluctant pilots, particularly in the late afternoon after the pubs had opened.

On the 9th of February, to our immense relief and delight, four of us were posted to No. 59 OTU, Operations Training Unit, at Grangemouth on the Firth of Forth in Scotland. This was an RAF station, all spit and polish and saluting, but with battle-proven instructors and a purposeful air. After filling out the usual forms and signing the usual documents, we were issued with flying boots, fleece-lined jacket, gloves, helmet, parachute and a locker to store them in. We had billets in a manor house in Avondale and went to and from by bus or on foot if you missed it, which no one did twice.

Ground school began on the 11th with the usual subjects—Navigation, Wireless, Armaments—plus stimulating new ones in Operations, Tactics, Aircraft Identification and Intelligence, or, what the Hun was doing. Flying started two days later, first with dual instruction on the Master, a nimble little trainer. After a forty-minute orientation flight, my instructor, P/O Matthews, let me go solo and it was amazing how easily it all came back after being earthbound for three months. The weather was duff the next day but on the 15th, after an hour alone in the Master and a ten-minute test by the Flight Commander, I was ready for the Spitfire. Cockily self-confident as always, I'd convinced my instructors that I merited being the first of the class to go skyward in the Spit 1A.

In two sessions that afternoon, P/O Matthews revealed the mysteries of this most feminine of all fighter aircraft with its delicate lines, dainty wheels and tiny cockpit. He gave me the gen on its flying characteristics, its quirks and foibles, and, standing on the wing with me inside, he went over and over the cockpit drill—ignition, throttle, patch, mixture, trim, rpm, etcetera. I repeated it until it became automatic though my mind was more on the thrills ahead than on these petty details. Finally Matthews said "Okay, take her away!" jumped off the wing and sauntered off.

I started the engine, called Control for permission to take off, taxied out toward the runway, jogging left and right to see ahead, and lined her up for the sky. Closed the hood, checked the instruments, pushed the throttle forward, and we were on our way.

But where was the roar they talked about, the tremendous acceleration that pushed you back in the seat? The Spit lumbered down the runway no faster than a Master and it made a noise like an old truck. Halfway down the speedometer was only at 80 but I thought it was about time to get airborne. I pulled the stick back. We inched up and clumped down again. I could see the fence and trees at the end of the runway were getting close and I began to worry. The throttle was fully forward but where was the power? I jammed the stick into my crotch and we went up again, down again, and then finally, after a bounce or two, we were a few feet in the air, just high enough to clear the boundary fence. I hauled up the undercarriage and, skimming the tree tops, started climbing. But oh so slowly, so painfully!

Watching the speed carefully so as not to stall I made a flat, slow turn to port. It was then I saw the red flares shooting up from the aerodrome and a fire-truck, speeding out to the runway. Control came on and in a strained voice ordered me to land immediately. This I intended to do as clearly something was wrong. I completed the circuit at 400 feet and fell onto the runway with a landing that almost sheered off the wheels.

When I taxied in Matthews jumped onto the wing. He was white-faced. "You bloody clot!" he shouted. "You took off in coarse pitch and you're bloody well still in it!" I looked at the pitch lever, which I'd totally forgotten, and was so ashamed I could have shot myself. A bit shaken too as I realized this solo in a Spitfire could have been my last flight ever. I was grounded for four days and was lucky not to have been grounded permanently.

I felt the Spit's power and acceleration when I took off the second time, on the 19th, this time in fine pitch, and the difference was like night and day as we bulleted into the sky. I was tempted to keep climbing but restrained myself as Matthews had said circuits and bumps only and I wanted no more blacks. After six landings, each one more passable than the last, I fell in love with this ravishing lady of the air, eager to go heavenward and cavort with her in loops, rolls and spins.

But aerobatics did not come, at least officially, until three weeks later. First there were basic exercises: local flying to find your way about, DF homings to get back to base when lost, and altitude climbs to familiarize yourself with the use of oxygen over 15,000 feet. Local flying could be hazardous as Grangemouth was in an industrial belt covered with smog and the aerodrome was in the thickest of it. The weather provided good experience in map reading under difficult conditions as well as in instrument flying as you were frequently compelled to call Control for a homeward course through the muck. Coming down after altitude climbs some of us did rolls, loops and even spins and, whenever far from base, equally unauthorized low flying on the pretext of identifying landmarks.

Most stimulating of the exercises was formation flying. We went up first in the Master with instructors who showed us how and then took their lives in their hands by letting us try. Four kites, line abreast, line astern or in Vics, flying straight and level and then climbing, diving and breaking, tucked in as close as you dared, wing tip on wing tip or prop shaving the tailplane of the one ahead. After that, alone in the Spit on flights of four, eight or twelve, tearing through the air glued together in ever more violent manoeuvres, sometimes breaking into imaginary Huns. Hours and hours of it and when you got back to base you were exhausted but exhilarated. Flying in formation demanded the utmost in concentration, fine judgement of speed and distance, delicate control of throttle, rudder and elevator, constant alertness and yet an inner calmness. It provided excellent training in aircraft handling and self-discipline and I came to enjoy it almost as much as aerobatics.

The master in aerobatics was the C/O, Squadron Leader Petrie, and he taught some of us the art in the Master. He made the old trainer do everything both in and outside the book: triple rolls, reverse rolls, rolls off the top, stalls in steep turns, recovery from spins at the last second, inversions at lowest level. Trying to imitate him was a lesson in humility. A lesson in self-confidence too as with him you gained the feeling of being an integral part of the plane, its body and wings your own. On the ground he gave us some timely advice. "It's fun, yes, but fun's not the object. It's not a Sunday show. You do that in the Spit to get at the Hun or to get away from him. And always remember: keeping looking around even while you're doing it!"

This lesson I learned on my first search and intercept exercise. I was flying formation with an instructor, Pilot Officer Smith, when he called, "Okay, you're the Hun and I'm the hunter. See if you can spot me before I shoot you down." He disappeared. I flew straight and level, weaving constantly and turning my head to see above, below and behind. He was up there in the sun I was sure, waiting to pounce, and I'd see him first and break before he got close. But the sky was empty—where was he? Suddenly Smith's lah-di-dah voice filled my ears. "I'm very much afraid, Red Two, you're dead, very dead indeed!" I broke but he was on my tail, zooming up from below in the middle of the blind spot! "You've got to weave, dear boy," he said laconically. "And look behind your fanny as well as behind your noggin!" He invited me to attack him but the closest I got was with a deflection shot from 300 yards or more. From that time on, whenever up alone, I weaved like a whirling dervish and swivelled my head until my neck got stiff, knowing it would later be a matter of life or death.

The exercises that followed were all operations-oriented: dogfighting, stern and quarter attacks with cine camera, formation interceptions and then, with guns, shooting at targets on the water or the drogue in the air. The drogue was a long canvas funnel towed over the sea by a Lysander and in quarter attacks you tried to fill it with holes. Piloting a Lysander was a dangerous occupation considering the erratic aims of student pilots. I sheered off the tow line twice and only toward the end put a few holes into the canvas.

Apart from the regular subjects there were lectures on tactics, parachute jumping, methods of escape in enemy territory and several sessions on the range, shooting at moving targets with a rifle. Ground School finished on March 15th and the only marks I could crow about were in aircraft identification. I should at least be able to recognize the Hun though I wondered if I'd ever get close enough to shoot one down.

When the course finished on the 12th of April I was satisfied to get an "Average" rating considering the black I'd pulled on the solo. I was posted to 421 Squadron at Digby, Lincolnshire, a new Canadian outfit just being formed. I'd hoped for a posting further south in 11 Group but felt I was in no position to protest.

CHAPTER II

The Welding of a Squadron in South Wales

Though Digby was well north of the happy hunting grounds of 11 Group it looked and felt like an operational station. Its officers' mess was well-worn, its dispersals scruffed up by countless pilots on readiness, its field noisy with aircraft flying to and from distant war fronts. And while 421 Squadron was brand new its seventeen Mark VA Spitfires were old and battle-scarred.

Its first Commanding Officer was S/L Fred Kelly, Canadian of Irish descent and temperament, formerly a Flight Commander of 402 Squadron. He had arrived on April 11th followed by his two Flight Commanders, F/L Jack Long and F/L George Hill, and the rest of the complement of twenty-three pilots straggled in over the next ten days. I was the seventh to report, keen as they to pass muster. The Engineering, Intelligence and Medical Officers did not come on strength until early May but fortunately for the C/O an early newcomer was the Adjutant, P/O Chasanoff, straight from Canada. Chubby, ebullient "Chas" proved to be an expert in both paper-pushing and scrounging, the latter a priceless asset for a new squadron short of supplies, parts and people.

Fred Kelly's first task was to get the seventeen clapped-out Spits serviceable. With borrowed staff and parts purloined by the new Adjutant he had most of them on line before the arrival of his own ground crew, one hundred and eight of them, split between RAF and RCAF. His second task, after the kites had been air tested, was to weld his fledgling pilots into the semblance of a team. This he initiated by leading them on formation flights, line astern and close up for show, spread out for battle. By the end of April the new-born squadron had logged in 930 hours, most on formation.

On the third of May 421 moved to its first permanent base at Fairwood Common on the south coast of Wales near Swansea, its duties to protect shipping from attack by German submarines and long-range bombers. It was replacing 402 Squadron, due to leave in ten days' time for the front-line base of Kenley in 11 Group.

The prospect of flying day after day on convoy patrols in a zone beyond reach by Hun fighters was so unappealing I asked Fred Kelly to post me to 402 before its departure. I knew he and the C/O of 402 were pals and I'd heard that one of the latter's pilots was being taken off, tour-expired. Over beer in the mess the two C/Os agreed to the switch and the following day I was on convoy patrol with a senior 402 pilot, my first operational sortie. But the dream of dogfights over France lasted only three days as Headquarters vetoed the transfer and I was moved back to 421. Fortunately the pilots in my Flight did not accuse me of disloyalty as, given the choice, they would have done the same.

So it was back to the working-up program of formation flying, simulated dog fights with camera and air-to-ground firing, preparatory to becoming operational. Spirits picked up considerably when on May 10th, a wet but happy Sunday, twelve new Mark VB Spitfires were flown in by factory pilots, some of them attractive young women. Within a week all of the old kites had been replaced by this improved Mark.

On May 14th 402 departed and 421 became operational, A and B Flights alternating on readiness from dawn to dusk. We yearned for calls from Control to scramble after Huns or unidentified aircraft but they came seldom and the daily chores were the tedious, frustrating convoy patrols. Every hour, the section of two on immediate readiness took off and on a course given by Control headed for the ships. We saw them, ten to twenty in a line, ploughing slowly west in the Bristol Channel or east from St. George's Channel further out. Replacing the section on patrol, we took up station at about 5,000 feet, the altitude dependent on the height of the cloud and visibility, and then cruised on lean mixture, line abreast and wide apart, back and forth parallel with the course of the convoy. We weaved constantly, looking to port and starboard, up above and to the rear, keeping an eye cocked always on our charges below. Wishing them no harm, we prayed that a Dornier or JU88 would appear so we could become heroes but the only aircraft encountered occasionally were bogeys—Blenheims or Beauforts returning from patrols further seaward. When relieved by another section we returned to base, dejected but a little consoled in knowing our efforts had achieved two objectives: preventative in keeping hostile aircraft away and psychological in helping to maintain the morale of the seamen below.

Though operational, the Squadron was still in training and half the air time was spent in cine-gun attacks, air-to-ground firing and formation. Every afternoon the C/O would lead the Flight not on readiness, or the whole Squadron when readiness was cancelled, in close formation several times across the aerodrome to get the criticism of the ground staff. Then in post-mortem sessions at the bar he'd tear strips off everyone. "Dammit, fellas," he'd say, "That was a squabble not a squadron formation and your nattering was like the quacking of scared ducks!" Under his jovial scolding air discipline quickly improved, the chattering ceased and the space between aircraft shortened, so much so that on one occasion the aerial of one kite punctured a hole in the wing of another, frightening both pilots but causing little damage. Accidents in this period were inevitable however: two crash landings, one due to engine failure, the other to shortage of petrol, and a near-fatal crash when a pilot forgot to switch on his oxygen and spun in 10,000 feet before regaining consciousness.

Fred Kelly knew that esprit de corps was the sine qua non of an effective fighting unit and he actively promoted it, in the air and on the ground. He joined in the card games and horseplay in flight dispersals, and after dinner in the mess he convened beer and bull sessions, commanding everyone to have a glass in hand even if it contained only ginger ale. Camaraderie going beyond distinctions of rank, he and his flight commanders frequently visited the sergeants' and airmen's messes for more beer and jollity. When the Squadron was not on readiness he encouraged "smashes" at local pubs where singing with the musical Welsh was the principal entertainment. We were getting to know each other, drunk and sober, and without our being aware of it a feeling of solidarity developed and we were becoming a team. It was a team brought fully up to strength when Ted Martin joined as Intelligence Officer, Don Brewster as Engineering Officer and "Doc" Cadham as Medical Officer. And always adding zest to every gathering was the irrepressible Chas Chasanoff.

A change of pace came in June when the Squadron was transferred to Exeter to take over readiness for a Czech squadron that had been moved temporarily elsewhere. Here, in addition to convoy patrols there were several scrambles that raised and dashed hopes, one that took my section almost to Ireland to clear the skies of mythical Huns. Then, relieved of patrols for eight days, we moved to the gunnery practice camp at Warmwell for a concentrated program of cine-gun and air-to-air firing exercises. My own scores being nothing to boast about, when we returned to Fairwood I volunteered for a four-week course at the Pilot's Gunnery Training Wing at Sutton Bridge in Lincolnshire, directed by Wing Commander "Sailor" Malan DSO DFC, a leading ace of the first years of the war.

There were ten pilots on the course from several commands including coastal, ranging in rank from Wing Commander to Pilot Officer. It was an intensive program monitored by instructors on which we flew four times a day, shooting with cannon and machine gun on drogue and ground targets and with camera on other Spits or groups of bombers, the latter exercise being as close to the real thing as one could get without bullets. Every evening the results were analyzed, pilot by pilot, in the main lecture hall. It was a sixteen-hour working day with no parties in the mess—though Sailor Malan was nearly always on hand to offer advice when pressed.

A quarter attack with cine-gun on Whitleys with "Gorby," a Polish veteran, almost brought grief. We were pulling out when there was a "woof" sound and my kite slowed up. I pushed the throttle fully forward but nothing happened and then I saw white smoke streaming out behind.

"You got glycol leak," Gorby drawled. "Better bail out or put her down."

When the engine lost its coolant it seized up or caught fire and as the temperature was off the clock I cut the switch. Dead silence. Having no great desire to bail out, I tightened the straps and looked around. We were at eight thousand feet, coming down fast, and the fields below were small with stone walls around them. I picked one, bigger than the others, green with grain. The wind being from the west I glided east, circling and slipping off, keeping an eye on the field. When I straightened out it looked smaller and the stone wall higher. Getting close and going too fast, I eased the stick back, then brought the nose level, and skimmed over the wall at about eighty. With a "wisshing" noise the Spit cut through the grain, slowed up fast and came to a stop just before the wall on the other side, the tail coming up and flapping back. I undid the straps, climbed out and waved to Gorby circling above. Apart from a bent prop and bashed forehead there was no serious damage but after-shock made me almost weep for a dead rabbit lying near the tail.

The course ended on July 22nd and the results were flattering to the ego—Average on two counts, Above Average in combat shooting and Excellent as marksman on the drogue. Modesty and shame were to come later on learning with chagrin that good scores came easier in practice than in battle when the wily Hun showed a marked reluctance to fly straight and be shot down.

The Squadron had been in action during my absence. On separate sorties on 6 July F/L "Robbie" Robertson, who had replaced George Hill as head of B Flight, had attacked and damaged a JU88 and a long-range Me 109. In the week following P/O Handley and Sergeant Clasper were credited with the same score on another JU88 trying to attack a convoy. There was other news as well. S/L Fred Kelly, who had done so much to whip the Squadron into shape, had been tour-expired and replaced by S/L Cam Willis, a Canadian from the RAF, an experienced leader, modest and with an air of quiet confidence.

Convoy patrols were still the order of the day but the arrival of summer weather brought some variety in activities. On July 27th Sergeants Omand and Myers scrambled to intercept a bogey, found a JU88 flying at 500 feet and attacked it repeatedly until it crashed into the sea. This was 421's first confirmed kill. On the 31st we moved to Harrowbeer in Devon, first to provide cover for air-sea rescue boats picking up pilots who had bailed out of a shot-up Wellington and then, with extra fuel tanks, to protect bombers returning from an attack on the submarine base at St. Malo. On the 16th of August the Squadron flew to Warmwell in Dorset to stand in for the Ibsley RAF Wing, absent for undivulged reasons. There were rumours of something big in the offing but it was not until the 20th that we learned of the Canadian raid on Dieppe. Over a six-day period we were on constant readiness, sent off on futile chases after suspected bandits and on patrols to cover warships. It was back-up, defensive work, leaving us frustrated about not getting over the beachhead.

On the 23rd, one day after our return to Fairwood, the Squadron recorded its first fatal accident. Don Iverach, on a cine-gun exercise, spun in from 6,000 feet and crashed near the base, no one knowing how he'd lost control.

While there were no encounters with the enemy in August and September, the Squadron rapidly built up operational hours in convoy, escort and Recco patrols, air-sea rescue searches and the always hopeful but always uneventful scrambles. On one dawn to dusk search by sections we scoured the sea without success for the crew of a Beaufighter who had ditched the previous night, and on other sorties we flew at wave-top searching for mines dropped by German bombers. On one of several scrambles bad weather forced my section to land and overnight at Angle, a desolate spot to the west where rumour had it the Squadron was due to be transferred. Other breaks from convoy patrols included an escort of a huge floating dock being towed slowly along the coast by tugs and a long chase after an elusive Hun that took my section again within sight of the Irish coast.

The most frustrating sorties in this period were our attempts to shoot down an uninvited Hun visitor. Nearly every afternoon when the sky was clear we'd see him flying at nearly 40,000 feet from the west to the east, dragging his white contrail behind him. He was a German spy, sizing up the weather and taking photos of military installations. Though sure he was beyond reach by Spitfires, the C/O persuaded Headquarters to let us have a try. As soon as the high-flyer was picked up on radar by Control we'd take off, climb as fast and as high as we could and have a shot at him as he passed by.

On September 9th, Met forecasting a few days of good weather, Cam Willis let me take Kennedy, Myers and Meldeau to the RAF base at Colerne near Bath where we'd be in a better position for the interception. There we went on immediate readiness and the next day at three the scramble order came through and the four of us took off. At full throttle we climbed to 34,000 feet, more as the altimeter froze, but the call had come too late as when we got close enough to see the Hun, a blue-grey dot ahead of his contrail, he was high above and five miles to the east. The strain on the engine produced my second glycol leak, forcing a shakey dead-stick landing at Charmy Down.

Back at Colerne I took Meldeau's kite and the three of us waited two days for another scramble. It came at two-thirty on the 12th and this time Control was on the mark. At 35,000 feet we could see the Hun well to the west as, throttles through the gate, we clawed the air barely moving, the perspex fogging up at the slightest turn, hands and feet frigid. The dot got bigger as it came toward us like a bullet but it was at least two thousand feet above. Madly, I pulled the nose higher, aimed vaguely ahead of the intruder and let go with a burst of cannon and machine gun, knowing the bullets would only fan the air. The Spit baulked like a horse, the nose came down and we went into a half spin. Recovering, I called the others and we returned to base, the experiment concluded. The valiant Spit VB could get beyond its rated ceiling, of this I was sure, but it could never get high enough to do battle with a German Met plane.

On September 19th I took a week's leave and, restless, crowded it with activity: one night of good food, cheery talk and a comfy bed at my landlady, Mrs. Hook's, one night of too much beer at the Crackers' Club, the fighter pilot's rallying point in Soho, a relaxing weekend in the country at the home of Garfield Weston, Canadian millionaire, and visits to relatives in Lancashire. Sad news greeted me on returning to Fairwood: Sergeant Mackay, 421's only American pilot, had lost control while flying formation in cloud and had crashed into a mountain, killing himself.

The thought of more convoy patrols was disheartening and so on the 16th of October when a call came through for volunteers to go to Malta, the island under daily attack by both Germans and Italians, Sergeant Goodwin and I jumped at it. Jack Long and Hap Kennedy had responded to an earlier call and were awaiting pre-departure briefing in London. We'd be flown to Gibraltar, board a carrier and, halfway across the Mediterranean, take off and fly the rest of the way to the besieged island, an exciting prospect.

But for me it was not to be. Two days before the briefing, while visiting the Argyles near Canterbury, the first stomach pains started and during the farewell party the following night at the Savoy, organized by Chasanoff who was then on leave, I spent most of the time vomiting in the w.c. The next morning, instead of attending the briefing, I was in an ambulance for a Canadian hospital in Surrey where a Colonel Macintosh removed a ruptured appendix. After ten days in hospital and three weeks' convalescence in Herefordshire I reported to RCAF Headquarters, hopefully for re-establishment of the Malta posting.

"Too late, you missed the boat," the posting chief said heartlessly. "You're going back to 421 as there've been changes and they need their old hands." The "old" made me feel like a has-been.

As I feared, the Squadron had been transferred to Angle, the RAF base near Milford Haven on the southwestern tip of Wales, as distant from the aerial battles of 11 Group as one could possibly get. When I arrived by truck from the railway station I couldn't see the airfield it was raining so hard and I had to search on foot for the officers' mess, an old manor house a long way from the field. I was far from cheerful when I reported there to the new commanding officer, S/L Fred Green DFC. He had replaced quiet and steady Cam Willis who during my absence had been shot down and killed with his number two, Sergeant Davis, while protecting Fortresses on their return from a bombing mission.

It was like joining a different outfit, there seemed to be so many new faces. Robbie Robertson still headed B Flight but a newcomer from 416 Squadron, F/L P.G. Blades, had taken over A Flight from Jack Long, now happily in Malta. Blades looked like a dour kind of chap and I wasn't too keen about being assigned to his Flight. As it turned out, we were to become lifelong friends.

Weather and not the Hun was the enemy at Angle in winter months. Nearly always there was cloud, often low and treacherous, greying out the line between sky and sea. Winds came from all points of the compass, sometimes at gale force that made landings tricky especially when rain or sleet blurred the runway. When the base of the cloud was low it was difficult to locate a convoy and to keep it in sight on patrol and, returning to base, we frequently had to call Control for a homing and were much relieved when in the last few seconds we saw the breakers against the cliff and edged our kites over. We flew in warm, bulky clothing, wondering how we'd get out if the engine failed, sure we'd sink like a stone if we did. Convoys must have felt safer in bad weather as there were a lot of them in December. There were a few scrambles after bogeys but mostly it was the dreary ushering of ships up and down St. George's Channel, even for some of us on Christmas Eve, Christmas and Boxing Day.

There was a plus side however to the winter weather of Angle as on the ground it herded us together for shelter and solace. We were the only permanent squadron on the station and this was another factor stimulating unity and social self-sufficiency. Except for the Globe Hotel in the village of Angle pubs were few and distant and so pilots and airmen found relaxation in dispersal huts and living quarters. For pilots the waiting hours on readiness in dispersals were spent playing cards, shooting darts, writing letters and listening to the non-stop gramophone. Glen Miller and Artie Shaw were honorary members of 421.

Esprit de corps was enhanced on long winter nights by the congenial atmosphere of the officers' mess, the manor house I'd thought so little of on arrival. The living room and bar with well-worn sofas, the cosy dining room and the bedrooms upstairs with fireplaces created a feeling more of a home than a military barracks. After dinner impromptu parties over beer started at any moment and on any pretext, usually ending up in singsongs, the old refrains becoming off-colour ditties after the two WAAF officers had retired to bed: "Roger of Kildare," "The Foggy, Foggy Dew," "Come Ki Yippi Yi," "No Balls at All" and others equally disreputable. On occasion there was a more organized party or station dance, ladies recruited miraculously by Chasanoff. Our special girlfriends however, shared platonically, were the WAAF transport drivers—Jean, Doreen, Glynis and Susie—and the operators of the wireless repeater station near the runway who, in evenings when on standby, invited us over, no more than three at a time, to share our food parcels and their cheerful company.

The bedrooms on the second floor of the mess were also centres of nocturnal festivity. Except for the C/O's room, each accommodated four to six officers, A and B Flights being separated to prevent or foster battles between them. Here dirty plots were hatched against one's rivals: to put worms or pepper in others' beds, tie sheets in knots, barricade entrances with chairs and other juvenile pranks as antidotes to boredom. And in these rooms on cold winter nights another competitive and enjoyable activity took place: the opening and sharing of parcels from home—parcels with delicacies such as spam, oysters, sardines, salmon, pork and beans, peanut butter, crackers, fruit cake, nuts and raisins—rooms vying with each other in the variety of their offerings. Songs were sung, jokes told, the world set aright, and it was on one of these festive nights that the decision was taken to write to McColl Frontenac for permission to use its emblem so that 421 could become "The Red Indian Squadron."

Robbie Robertson's room, shared with three of his pilots and Don Brewster, the Engineering Officer, claimed the title for notoriety as it was here the "Anti-Farting Club" was established, its rules and privileges posted on the door. You could have one for sixpence, six for half a crown, an open evening for ten shillings. And it was in this room on one evening close to Christmas that the WAAF drivers were smuggled in by ladder to share a parcel feast, later to be hidden under the beds when the stuffy RAF Station Adjutant came to investigate the sound of female laughter. He was diverted by a triple whiskey offered by pilots faking girlish giggles at the door.

On Christmas Day everyone celebrated with utter abandon, the weather co-operating in allowing only three operational flights. At noon the officers, suitably primed, served dinner for the airmen in their mess and then repaired to their own for a turkey banquet, the singing of carols and a station dance to the music of the airmen's orchestra, whose members were as well-oiled as the dancers. In the history of Angle this day-long "thrash" was recorded as the most hilarious.

But if duff weather and geographic isolation were the prime stimulants of conviviality it was the character of 421's leadership that contributed most to its harmonious spirit. The four ground officers were genial and supportive: wise custodian of physical and mental health, Doc Cadham; competent Engineering Officer, Don Brewster; tactful Intelligence Officer, Ted Martin; and the inimitable Chas Chasanoff, scrounger, fixer, comedian, without doubt the most unorthodox Adjutant in the RCAF. The two Flight Commanders, Phil Blades and Robbie Robertson, completely different in personality, were excellent pilots and perfectly-cast lieutenants of the C/O. Phil, or "Peegee," was taciturn, serious but with a wry sense of humour, his feelings always under control. When leading his Flight his dry voice on the radio, never hurried, gave everyone confidence. Robbie on other hand was a buoyant, waggish extrovert and a good-humoured prankster. Like Phil, in the air he was deliberate and unflappable but on the ground the only predictable thing about him was his unpredictability. Both were admired and respected by their pilots.

The unquestioned pace-setter of the Squadron was the C/O, Freddy Green, "Da Chief" as he was often called. Speaking in a drawl, walking with a slouch, pipe constantly in his mouth, always grinning, Freddy had a charismatic air about him. A good story teller, he was the author of the Squadron's most colourful expressions, mostly off-colour. He exuded calmness and good cheer, led without making an effort to do so, and enjoyed the loyalty of pilots and ground crew.

———

During a storm on the night of January 1st a convoy out of Liverpool was attacked by submarines and two ships were sunk. The following day, while B Flight remained on readiness, A Flight was sent in sections of two to help look for survivors. When Al Fleming and I reached our assigned area, far out in St.

George's Channel, we started a north-south search at 5,000 feet. The storm had abated but the sea was still high and it was cold.

Near the end of the first leg south we saw a small coastal freighter heading in the same direction, surprisingly alone. We flew a bit beyond it, turned west for one minute and then headed back north, tipping the wings to look below. Suddenly I saw, or thought I did, a spot on the sea that was more than a crashing wave. Signalling Fleming, I dived down and at 1,000 feet the spot became a small boat, at 200 feet an open lifeboat with two men in it, one lying motionless in the middle, the other slouched at the stern, looking up. He waved an arm slowly as if it was an effort to do so and I wagged my wings.

Thinking of the ship we'd seen, I climbed back to 5,000 feet and called Control, telling them we'd try to divert it to the rescue. While Fleming remained circling to give Control a fix and me a return point I flew full throttle on an estimated course for the freighter. When I saw it I dropped down and flew on a parallel course to identify myself, wagging my wings. Flying at fifty feet I circled the ship and saw two men on the bridge, one with binoculars. I circled again, waving a hand forward as I passed, and headed north in the direction of the lifeboat, hoping the man with the binoculars would see my signal. I repeated the manoeuvre a second time, pulling the hood open, my open hand going back and forth. There was no reaction. Frustrated, I made a third try and this time, passing the ship, I pressed the gun button for four or five seconds and bullets sprayed the water. That did it, as when I flew back the ship stopped, turned fast and reversed its course.

I wagged my wings joyously and started leading the way, calling Fleming to inform Control of what was happening. After thirty minutes of flying back and forth like a whippet coaxing a tortoise I saw Fleming circling ahead and he called to report seeing the freighter ploughing the waves at full speed behind me. We circled together until it was within two hundred yards of the lifeboat and then, concerned about shortage of petrol, headed back to base. The two seamen were picked up but we never did learn whether the one in the middle survived the ordeal.

The weather worsened, with high winds and snow in early January but spirits were high as first a rumour and then an oral report forecast an early transfer of 421 to 11 Group. To get the outfit into shape for the move the C/O ignored the weather and led the Squadron or elements of it in formation flying in cloud and on the deck, persuaded the army to provide targets for air-to-ground firing and an army co-operation unit to tow a drogue for air-to-air, organized dogfights with cine-gun, low flying map reading and, on one night without cloud, night flying practice to and from Fairwood. The oral report was soon confirmed: the Squadron would replace 412 at Kenley on January the 29th. The waiting days, though busy ones, passed with agonizing slowness. Then, on the 24th, there was another fatal accident.

Phil Blades was leading four of his pilots in formation practice above Milford Haven when one of them, Sergeant Alex Aitken, misjudged his distance and in a turn sheered off the propeller of Phil's plane with his starboard wing, losing the end of it. Alex turned toward base but spun in and crashed near the runway, killing himself on impact. Without prop, Phil glided toward land but seeing he wasn't going to make it pulled back the hood and prepared to ditch, tricky in a Spit as the Merlin engine in front was like a heavy anchor that pulled the kite to the bottom in a flash. A wing tip touched the sea first, delaying the sinking by precious seconds. He banged the harness release, freed himself from parachute and Mae West, and squeezed out of the cockpit when it was under water. Swimming to the surface he headed for the shore, the current against him. Fortunately two army men had witnessed the ditching and rushed down to pull him to safety.

In keeping with custom, there were drinks at the bar that night for Alex, as well as for Phil on his escape. He, a light-drinking man, was forced to down several double whiskies and while under their influence attacked the unpopular Station Adjutant with a soda siphon, chasing him out of the dining room and up the stairs to the safety of his room. His theatrical black, for which he was nicknamed "Leggsy," was suitably recorded in 421 annals. Alex's funeral was held in the village church two days later, attended by all ranks not on duty and by three WAAFs from the repeater station, there to comfort one of their numbers, Anne, Alex's nineteen-year-old fiancé.

The final going-away party was held on the night of January 28th, a riotous affair that drove the Station Commander and all other RAF personnel to their beds for security. They must have heaved a collective sigh of relief when early the following morning two Harrows arrived to take the wild Canadians to Kenley. Most of the ground crew had gone by lorry and train and the aircraft were being left for the incoming squadron. This was fortunate as our state of glorious inebriation did not guarantee much safety behind the joystick of a Spitfire.

No. 2 ITS Regina, May 1941. Art Sager third from left, second row.

Jay Stevens, Saskatoon. A bit more than a sister.

Blind date, friend, then wife, Dorothy Planche, November.

On readiness in beaten-up Spit 5A, Fairwood Common, 1942.

First fatal accident. Don Iverach spins in from 6,000 feet.

Officers' Mess, an old manor house, Angle, Southwest Wales.

The two jolly WAAF officers, protectors of their flock, Angle.

Two unprotected WAAFs smuggled into Robbie's room.

Weather was the enemy at Angle.

The Red Indians at Kenley, March 1943. S/L Freddy Green with pipe.

"Spartan" exercise, rehearsal for invasion, planes marked as friend or foe.

Redhill. S/L Hall seated second from right, PG and AS either side.

P.G. "Leggsy" Blades caught napping, Redhill.

The double wedding; fortunately the Squadron was grounded.

My B Flight ground crew, Kenley.

"Piddling" Pete criticizing a take-off.

416 Squadron dispersal, Digby. S/L Green centre, F/L Doug Booth on his right.

Dave Harling, in Mae West, later 416's C/O, killed in heroic action on 1 January 1945.

Ramrod 290 over Schipol. The seven who shot down nine in nine minutes.

Hit by 20 mm shell on aborted rhubarb to Zuider Zee.

CHAPTER III

Hunting the Hun Under W/C Johnnie Johnson

I thought I was in heaven when I woke up that first morning at Kenley. Opening my eyes, I saw an angel leaning over me, a beautiful angel with blue eyes. She was saying, "Sir! Sir! Your tea, Sir!" I reached up but she sprang away and flew out of the room. It was a WAAF batswoman, a new one, this her first day on duty. Unable to arouse me by knocking she'd come right in with the morning tea. A delightful Kenley custom but sadly the only time I was served it in bed.

There were other attractive features of Kenley, a Battle of Britain base in Surrey, thirty minutes by train from London. The officers' mess had a double lounge, one with a piano and the other with a bar, a huge dining room, a theatre for briefings, movies and concerts, a billiard room, gymnasium and squash court. The bedrooms in the main building and annex were single-occupancy, and in addition to bringing tea in the morning a batswoman or batman shined your shoes if they were left outside overnight. The meals were plentiful and tasty—porridge, sausages, kippers, frequently eggs for breakfast—and dinners of pre-war variety. Nothing but the best for fighter pilots on front-line service. The only drawback, a minor one, was the distance from mess to dispersals, forcing everyone to acquire a bicycle or motorbike.

When we arrived there were three other Canadian squadrons on the station—402, 403 and 416—but this imposed no strain on its extensive facilities. The original plan had been for 421 to occupy Redhill, the satellite a few miles south, but as its grass field was sodden from winter rains for a few weeks we were obliged to share the luxuries of the parent base with our sister outfits. Group Captain "Iron Bill" McBrien, a popular Canadian, was Station Commander and the Wing was led by Wing Commander "Johnnie" Johnson DSO, DFC and Bar who was to become the highest-scoring fighter pilot in the RAF.

We had inherited 412's Spit Mark VBs but it took a week to get them all serviceable. We were immediately reminded, however, that we were on more active operations when briefed by the Wing Intelligence Officer on action to be taken if forced to bail out or crash land in enemy territory. We were photographed in civilian clothing for identity cards to be used if downed and evading capture, and issued with escape kits containing silk map, phrase book in four languages and survival supplies. We were also given a P.38 revolver to protect ourselves in emergencies, not described.

Apart from occasional scrambles after intruders most operations from Kenley were circuses, rodeos, ramrods and road-steads. A circus was an escort of light bombers with the main purpose of luring the Hun into the air rather than of bombing; a rodeo, a sweep without bombers also to draw the enemy into action; a ramrod, an escort of a large-scale bombing mission within the limits of the Spitfire's range; a roadstead, the protection of bombers attacking ships at sea or in harbour. Briefings for these missions took place about an hour before "tit pressing" and takeoff, the Wing Commander giving information on the type of show and on the target if it was an escort job, on the role and tactics of the Wing and each squadron, on courses and timing. Watches were synchronized. The Intelligence Officer advised on possible enemy reaction, amount of flak to be expected and action to be taken if shot down or in trouble while the Met man gave a forecast of the weather en route. Briefings were concluded by the Wingco's rallying remarks—a coach urging on his team before the whistle.

The waiting between briefing and takeoff was the most edgy time, at least for the first shows, and to keep calm you fussed over your kite with your rigger and fitter. Once in the air you were too busy to be nervous. Squadrons took off in formation, formed up as a wing outside the circuit and then flew just above the treetops for the Channel. Crossing the English coast you switched on the gun button and reflector sight and, climbing, the Wing rendezvoused at the scheduled time and altitude with the bombers, each squadron taking up its assigned position at high, close or rear cover and its three sections spread out in loose formation.

My first operation was a rodeo, a wide sweep from Hardelot to Dunkirk, the Wing Commander leading 421, presumably to size us up. It was a clear morning with only a few clouds and we could see the French coast as soon as we started climbing to 19,000 feet. 403 were on our port slightly below, 416 above to starboard. As we crossed over Hardelot flak appeared on the left coming from Boulogne, grey-black puffs bursting like blossoms, closest to 403 but they didn't budge. The country below looked peaceful in the morning sunlight, its fields a multi-coloured patchwork of greens and browns.

We'd kept radio silence since takeoff and my head snapped back when the voice came on.

"Hello, Greycap Leader, Grass-seed here. Do you read me?" It was the chief controller with his casual voice and Oxbridge accent.

"Loud and clear, Grass-seed," the Wingco replied.

"There are ten plus bandits to the right of you, now at 8,000 and climbing south."

"Thanks, Grass-seed, we'll investigate," Johnnie said, then adding, "Okay chaps, keep a look out. Turning starboard, now." After the turn the sun was on our left and behind, a good spot if the Huns were ahead and below.

Minutes went by, the squadrons spread out, everyone searching the sky. Then control came back on.

"Hello Greycap Leader, Grass-seed here. Sorry, but the rascals seem to have vanished."

"Damn," the Wingco grunted. "Thanks, Grass-seed, we'll get them another time."

Giving the order, he turned port and the Wing resumed the sweep, going over St. Omer to provoke a reaction from this enemy-infested base. The Huns didn't bite and I wondered if we weren't scaring them off with thirty-six aircraft. Would they have come up if we were only twelve?

We turned north and after ten or fifteen minutes encountered more flak, this time from Dunkirk, 403 again the intended victim. Making a wide sweep east we avoided it but didn't lose height until well in the clear over the Channel. It was a dull, routine show for the old hands but pleasantly exciting for me, whetting the appetite for more.

Another type of operation was a rhubarb, a low-level intrusion into enemy territory usually by a section of two aircraft to search out and shoot up military targets such as locomotives, freight cars, army vehicles and gun installations. Rhubarbs were carried out only in duff weather when the Spits could nip into cloud if set upon by superior numbers of Hun fighters. And they were strictly voluntary. Most squadron leaders felt the damage done did not warrant the risks involved though they usually yielded if you put up a good plan and if they thought you needed to work off excess energy.

I badgered Ted Martin, the Squadron Intelligence Officer, until he eventually suggested trying the railway line from Rouen to Dieppe on which the underground had reported regular traffic of ammunition trains supplying German batteries at the coast. P/O "Peewee" McLachlan and I decided to give it a try, and the C/O ceding the green light, we worked out a course that would take us over a lightly defended stretch of the French coast west of Treport, then south to the railway going out of Rouen and back north along it to Dieppe. We took off at ten-thirty on February 15th, on a drizzly morning with cloud at 500 feet, perfect rhubarb weather.

The cloud base was lower and the rain heavier as we skimmed the Channel line abreast, hoping our navigation was accurate. Miraculously it was: at the calculated time we roared over barren cliffs into the peaceful farmland of Normandy. At a hundred feet we flew, more slowly now, over fields, woods, roads and hamlets, dipping into valleys and topping small hills, keeping an eye out for power lines and looking for anything military. We almost missed the railway as it was in a cut but got back over it and started north. Two minutes along the line a train appeared, coming our way, its engine puffing smoke, a passenger train with four small carriages.

"Too bad, Mac, it's not for us!" I muttered into the mike.

There was nothing else on the line, no freight cars or locomotives even in two industrial areas. Concentrated on searching, I suddenly realized we were on the outskirts of Dieppe, too late to change course. I called for full throttle and we zoomed over the town and harbour, seeing splashes in the water from the one gun that had swung around, fortunately too late. My fitter and rigger were disappointed when they saw the guns hadn't been fired and I almost regretted not having shot up the engine of the passenger train. The next day Kinnaird and Goudie, on a rhubarb further west, got six locomotives, though Goudie was lucky to get back as his kite was full of holes from AA guns.

Despite unstable weather there were a good number of wing shows in February, most escorting Venturas or Bostons serving as decoys or attacking shipping, all encountering nothing but unfriendly flak. Some of the bombers were hit though all made it safely home. On a circus with Venturas to Cherbourg and Caen, the Northolt Wing, flying with us, scared off a gaggle of Huns but lost one of their own. On a roadstead with twenty-four Venturas to Dunkirk 402 and 403 tangled with twenty plus Me 109s, destroying two and damaging others though one of their pilots failed to return. Now 2 I.C., second in command, and occasionally leading the Flight, I had yet to get close enough to the enemy to discover if I'd learned how to shoot.

One day of unflyable weather when the Wing was grounded there was an amusing diversion: an "evasion" exercise to test how we could manage if shot down over enemy territory. Without papers and money and disguised in civilian clothing as escaped Germans, all the pilots of the Wing were taken by lorry to points within ten miles of the station, dropped off and challenged to get back without being detected. The police, Home Guard and army were alerted, ordered to imprison would-be escapers, and the guards at the base were doubled. Acting experience giving a certain advantage, I talked myself into two rides, the first with a very kind elderly couple and the second with a lorry driver delivering food supplies to the officers' mess at Kenley. I told him I was AWOL, trying to sneak back without being stopped by the guard and he, sympathizing, agreed to collaborate if I kept his aid secret. Hidden under sacks of potatoes, I was driven to the station, climbed out and walked into the I/O's office, time between drop-off and return being fifty-six minutes. 421 took the prize with four pilots getting back undetected but it took hours to collect the scores of pilots lingering in jails and army barracks.

In late February 421's inimitable Adjutant, Chas Chasanoff, was promoted and transferred to a higher post elsewhere. His departure left a void which the older hands felt most deeply. He was replaced by F/O Claud Angus, a less colourful character but one whose competence we came to appreciate.

During the first ten days of March the Squadron participated with squadrons from other wings in an army co-operation exercise called "Spartan." Moving from one temporary airfield to another, living in tents and surviving on field rations, we provided cover for bombers against "enemy" fighters and attacked ground targets ahead of army units advancing out of a "bridgehead." Fighters and bombers were painted with vivid markings to distinguish "friend" from "foe" and cine-guns replaced both bullets and bombs. It was a rehearsal for the invasion of the continent which some thought imminent and, presaging what was to come a year later, the invading forces were the "winners" according to official observers.

The weather turned sour again in the latter part of the month and there were only a few operations, including patrols of convoys in the Channel, a circus with Bostons to Abbeville and a ramrod to protect masses of Fortresses and Liberators returning after a heavy mauling from a bombing raid into Germany. Because of the number of bombers involved several fighter wings were assigned to the task and they succeeded in driving off hordes of Messerschmitts and Focke Wulfs attacking the shattered formations, 604 Squadron losing four pilots in the battle. 421 at high cover was called into the fray but the best we could manage were a few long distance shots at fleeing Huns.

On March 24th the Squadron moved to the satellite base of Redhill, taking up sole occupancy of its grass field, dispersals and living quarters. The officers' mess, a manor house on a country estate, was more spacious than the mess at Angle but it had the same homey feeling about it. Mess "thrashes" were as uninhibited as usual but the one dance organized during our stay was a toned-down affair in keeping with the sedate atmosphere of Surrey. Transport still being a problem, more motorbikes were acquired, though returning from pubs by bike in the blackout could be as risky as being in a dogfight over France.

The major social event in this period was a double wedding, probably the only one in a Canadian fighter squadron in England during the war. P/O "Toddy" Todd and P/O "Issy" Isbister had fallen in love with WAAFs Valerie Newton and Vicky Hurtle respectively and on the last Saturday in March they tied the knots at the Kenton Methodist Church in Wimbledon. The Squadron had been grounded for the occasion and everyone attended though it was doubtful if all remembered being there.

Fortunately the preacher was a good sort who accepted the lack of solemnity in the church and who shared the hilarity of the reception that followed. It was a morale uplifting event enjoyed by both primary and secondary participants.

April marked the first anniversary of 421, now officially the "Red Indian Squadron" with an Indian head on the fuselage and "On The Warpath" the motto. But the month started badly. On the 1st F/Sgt Kinnaird failed to return from a rhubarb to the Carentan area and on the 3rd F/O Hal Rogers flipped over and was killed on a squadron takeoff.

Changes were occurring in personnel. Popular Freddie Green, "Da Chief," was tour-expired and replaced by S/L Jimmy Hall who quickly gained support by his quiet, confident manner. Three weeks later Robbie Robertson, O/C of B Flight, was posted, also tour-expired, and having seniority I moved pro tem into his place. Because of postings and losses only six of the original complement of pilots remained and the welding of a new team required another round of working-up exercises, at Redhill and for ten days at the gunnery practice camp at Martleshame Heath in Suffolk.

Full operational status was regained in early May when, with improved weather, wing shows increased, becoming daily by mid-month. But despite constant needling by circuses and ram-rods German fighters responded infrequently and when some did try to bounce the bombers they nearly always turned tail on sighting the Spits. A circus with Bostons to Cherbourg attracted only heavy flak though accurate enough to hole some of our kites, and while another circus with Venturas to Abbeville two days later brought up a dozen Me 109s, they were on their backs and away before we could get into them. P/O Cam Myers, number four in my section, went missing on this show. Not hearing or ignoring the C/O's order to return, he continued after the disappearing Huns and was either shot down or hit by flak.

On the 17th of May the Squadron moved back permanently to Kenley to replace 416 which had been transferred to Digby. We were delighted to return to the main base and even more delighted to acquire 416's Spit IXs. According to those who had tested it in combat this more powerful Mark was every bit as good as the current Me 109s and FW 190s. Of all Spitfire models it was to become my favourite. My contentment was made complete by being confirmed as commander of B Flight, the loyalty and keenness of its pilots being a tonic.

When taking over the Kenley Wing Johnnie Johnson had replaced line astern section flying by finger-four formation which provided more flexibility, better rear cover and more opportunity for all pilots to bring their guns into action. Its effectiveness was repeatedly demonstrated. On a circus with Venturas to Zeebrugge on the last day of May twenty FW 190s rose to the bait. 421 was closest and Jimmy Hall, ordering my section to give cover, led the other two into the attack. Half of his eight pilots fired their guns, destroying one and damaging others. As the C/O and his group pulled out my section entered the fray, lining up two 190s that had broken away in a turn to starboard. We whirled around after them but before we could get close enough they half-rolled and plunged like bullets into the smog. This was not the first nor the last time I shared the bewildering experience of milling about with friend and foe and then suddenly finding the sky completely empty of aircraft. In this case I still had the others with me; they'd stuck like glue throughout the violent manoeuvring.

May had been busy but June was busier, the logbook recording fifteen ramrods, five rodeos, two circuses and two convoy patrols as well as my first scores—if damaging an enemy aircraft and perhaps scaring its pilot could be so dignified. On a rodeo on the first of June 421 and 403 mixed it up with 109s and 190s without getting a single claim but on the 11th, on another rodeo, the C/O attacked twelve 109s over Abbeville, shooting down one and getting another as probable. Close behind on the port I chased three diving in a spiral, letting go with short bursts at the leader. There were strikes on the wing root and then smoke but he kept going. As others in my section confirmed the strikes I was credited with a damaged but I was dissatisfied with my leadership as we should have got all three. Four days later on a ramrod with Fortresses to Fecamp, the Wingco shot down two 109's, S/L Godefroy one, F/O Macdonald got a probable and, me, again off the mark, another damaged, this time confirmed by film. It was obvious the only way I was ever going to get a real score was to fly right up their tails.

On the 17th of June 421 had the misfortune to lose a second commanding officer. In the morning Jimmy Hall was tour-expired and replaced immediately by S/L Phil Archer who moved over from 402. That afternoon there was a rodeo to Dunkirk and Ypres and a huge armada of Germans rose up to do battle. In the ensuing dogfights both Archer and his number two, McNamara, were shot down. The Wing was credited with three destroyed and I had shots at two, hitting one I thought but not claiming, missing the other and considering myself lucky to have avoided bullets and other aircraft, friendly and unfriendly.

Two days later, S/L "Buck" McNair DFC, Flight Commander in 416, took over the Squadron and inaugurated his command by shooting down an Me 109 on his first show, a circus with Bostons to Abbeville from which three pilots of 403 failed to return. Buck was an excellent pilot and marksman, a blunt, rough character but intrepid air leader.

The four-engine, heavily-armed American Fortresses were increasingly replacing Bostons, Venturas and other light bombers on daylight raids. Carrying jettisonable extra fuel tanks, Spitfire wings escorted them to and out of Germany where the longer-range Mustangs took over while continuing to give them exclusive cover for attacks on targets in northern France, Belgium and Holland. The Forts flew at around 20,000 feet, in boxes of twenty or so, closely bunched for maximum protection by their gunners, following a leader who identified the target and marked it with incendiary bombs. While the bombsight of the Fortresses was highly accurate the navigational skill of their pilots left much to be desired, at least during the early months of their operations. Often the cascade of bombs in beautifully close patterns would fall on open fields or on targets other than the pre-selected one. Another weakness of the Forts, one of considerable concern to us, was in aircraft identification. Their gunners were seemingly unable to distinguish between Spitfires and Messerschmitts and they blasted away at both with unrestrained impartiality. Eventually we were ordered to remain 2,000 yards from our charges with their nimble-fingered gunners. On one occasion I could not and came home with a .5mm hole in the wing.

On June 27th the three squadrons of the Wing hovered protectively yet warily around a hundred Fortresses returning from a bombing raid to the Ruhr. They'd suffered heavy losses and their gunners were twitchy. Control reported fifteen plus bandits but they scurried away on seeing the Spits and we couldn't go after them as we had to keep the Wing intact to cover a score of stragglers. Equally frustrating was a ramrod the following day to bomb the marshalling yards at Bernay. When the second box of Forts failed to make the rendezvous the first box turned for home and we were ordered to see it safely across the Channel, having to ignore the thirty Huns reportedly rising to challenge us over France. Contact with the enemy was made however on two of the three ramrods on the 24th when two were destroyed though 403 lost one pilot and F/O Litton, hit in error by another Spit, was forced to crash land on a beach near Lympne.

There were five shows in the last five days of June, the first a shaky do on which the Wing climbed through thick cloud to 15,000 feet to rendezvous with Bostons heading for Holland. As there were no breaks in the cloud they had to abort and return with bombs aboard. On a ramrod with about fifty Fortresses to Tricqueville a dozen or more Me 109s attacked the leading bombers but were driven off by the concentrated fire of their nose gunners. Some of the Wing got close to the intruders before they found refuge in cloud but in the chase through the white stuff S/L Godefroy of 403 and his number two collided. The C/O got home but F/O Bowen was forced to bail out over enemy territory.

On a rodeo to St. Omer on the 27th a gaggle of aggressive FW 190s came up and in the dogfight Johnnie Johnson got another destroyed while I almost got my comeuppance. When closing in with my section on four Huns, Bob Heeney, flying number 4, called a break but there was so much chatter on the radio I didn't hear it. My first sight of danger, on looking around for the rest of the section, was coloured tracers from the guns of a 190 about a hundred yards behind. I was lucky as he, like me, was a bad shot. I yanked the stick back and pulled around in a stall turn and when I straightened out the sky was clear of friend and foe. I caught up with the Squadron when it was halfway home.

The busier you were in the air the more you needed to relax on the ground. You were living at a notched up level and to retain balance you had to unwind fully, if necessary intemperately.

I unwound on slightly inebriated visits to London though more often found relaxation in the companionship of dispersals and the mess. Johnnie Johnson was an enthusiast of body contact sports and sometimes organized noisy, brutal games of wall rugby in the main lounge, less brutal when well primed with beer. But there were other less vigorous forms of diversion—poker, snooker, movies or, most frequently, bull sessions around the bar. Anything to keep the mind clear of serious thoughts, of tomorrow or of loved ones. You might talk about tactics but never about the war; the cause was right and that was enough. Besides, there was no room in a Spitfire for a pacifist.

It often struck me that the qualities of an effective fighter pilot were not those of a responsible citizen in peacetime. Being in a killing game with death a close option you had to be thick-skinned, callous and ruthless. On the other hand what sustained you were the finer qualities of comradeship, loyalty and a sort of self-effacing dedication to the job, bloodthirsty though it was.

The logbook recorded eight rodeos and six ramrods during the first two weeks of July on which the Wing destroyed eight, got one probable and damaged four. On a rodeo on the morning of July 6th 421 mixed it up with a dozen 109s, the C/O getting one and me a damaged, though after seeing the strikes on film I convinced myself he'd have had trouble getting home. On the 9th we were taken back to Battle of Britain days when 421, on readiness, scrambled after Dorniers bombing Croydon at low altitude. We whizzed around through thick smog and friendly flak but couldn't find the bandits though two were reported downed by anti-aircraft gunners. There were raids by Fortresses on targets in the Paris area on both the 10th and 14th. On the first S/L Buck McNair destroyed one while I made two separate attacks, missing completely on one and generously credited with a damaged on the other. But why wouldn't they blow up?

On July 10th Phil "Peegee" Blades, O/C of A Flight, was hauled, protesting, off operations, tour-expired. I was glad he was grounded as he'd had a long first tour and was beginning to take unnecessary risks, a sure sign of being tired. We'd become close friends and his departure left a gap. It also raised questions in my mind about both the nature of leadership and the emphasis given to judging fighter pilots by their scores in combat. Good marksmen shot down Huns and were deservedly rewarded by DFCs but I felt that good pilots had other important qualities unrecognized by decorations. Courage was one of them and pilots needed an extra dose of it when they knew their shooting was not the best. All twelve pilots in a squadron played vital roles on operations—searching the skies for the enemy, attacking and breaking up enemy formations, protecting leaders against rear attack. Good leaders did their jobs when they led their pilots calmly into action so that as many as possible could have shots at the enemy. On the ground they instilled enthusiasm and confidence in their men. Blades was this kind of pilot and leader.

I was enjoying being a Flight Commander and all was going well in spite of my measly score when, suddenly, in the last week of July, my world fell apart. I pulled a black which almost ended my career in the Air Force.

I pulled it from the very best of intentions. I'd always felt that the ground crews, on whose diligence and skill our lives depended, were too often taken for granted and after taking over B Flight I spent as much time as possible with the Flight Sergeant and his men to show interest in their work and buck up their morale. On Saturday, July 17th, when the Wing was grounded because of thick cloud over the continent, I decided to remain on the station and take any of the ground crew who wanted on short flips in the Tiger Moth. Though the weather was foul in France it was a warm, sunny day in England. Eight of the ground crew including the Flight Sergeant put their names on the list to go up for a ride that afternoon.

I discovered later that it was not just the flight they were interested in. They'd heard some of the pilots talking about a nudist colony in the valley just east of the aerodrome, heard them boasting about seeing naked ladies cavorting on lawns and beside a swimming pool. Feeling cheated, they pleaded with me to take them over the erotic garden of Eden. I agreed though I knew the pilots' reports of delectable views were more imaginary than real; preoccupied as they were with instruments on take-offs and landings they were not able to see much of the forbidden fruit.

Not mentioning the nudists, I informed Flight Control of my plans and was given the green light for eight take-offs and landings roughly within the circuit. There was a light breeze from the east and after taking off on each flight I stayed low and then turned left to skim over the trees and the nudist colony, an open, park-like area. All my passengers were delighted as, leaning dangerously out of the cockpit goggle-eyed, they did indeed see a good deal of pink and white flesh about which they in turn were to boast gleefully later. From the point of view of morale this part of the afternoon outing was highly successful.

To prolong each flight so the ground crew could see as much as possible I made a wide swing on the down leg and flew at about 500 hundred feet over the attractive Surrey countryside.

At the western end I turned slowly and headed back to base. As we lost altitude we went over playing fields where some sort of sporting event was in progress. Had I been more alert I'd have noticed that on each flypast of the noisy Moth many of the children stopped in their running and jumping to wave but, foolishly as it was to turn out, I paid little heed to the distraction we were causing. After landing on the final sortie the Flight Sergeant and his men thanked me profusely and took me to the Airmen's mess for beer.

Three days later I was ordered to report to Group Captain McBrien, the Station Commander. He looked grim.

"Were you flying a Tiger Moth on Saturday, July 17th?" he asked in a formal tone of voice.

I replied affirmatively, saying I'd taken some of my ground crew for flips in the circuit.

"And did you fly, low and repeatedly, over St. Thomas School during its Annual Sports Day?"

I confessed that I had seen some kind of sporting event when making long approaches back to the field.

"Well, I'm sorry, Art," the Groupie said in a more friendly voice, "but you're in serious trouble. You've stirred up a hornet's nest at the Air Ministry. The Chairman of the Board of St. Thomas School is a prominent member of the Conservative Party and he has demanded that a Court of Enquiry be set up to take disciplinary action against the pilot who disrupted the sports day and endangered the lives of children. I have no alternative but to ground you for a week until the Court has made its ruling."

Shaken by this news, I left the station in disgrace and spent the week with friends living nearby while the unknown members of the Court of Enquiry carried out their investigations. I was somewhat comforted on learning through the grapevine that Flying Control had maintained I'd done normal circuits and that all my eight passengers had denied seeing anything of a sporting event.

At the end of the week I returned to the base and was allowed to lead the flight on two shows, a rodeo to St. Omer and a ramrod to Zeebrugge. Then, on July 28th, I was called back to the Station Commander.

"The Court of Enquiry has dismissed the case for lack of evidence," McBrien said. "And you can thank your friends in Flying Control and your ground crew for stretching the truth."

I blessed both secretly and heaved a sigh of relief.

"But—and I'm very sorry, Art—that's not the end of it. The Air Ministry is still under pressure and have insisted that some disciplinary action be taken." He paused, then went on. "They've ordered me to relieve you of your command, reduce you in rank, and post you to another station."

I suddenly felt nauseated, unable to believe his words. It wasn't the dropping of a stripe that hurt but losing my flight and leaving the Squadron

"I'm transferring you to 416 Squadron in Chad Chadburn's Wing at Digby," the Group Captain said. "Chad has been informed of the situation and has agreed to take you." He stood up.

"Goodbye and good luck!" he said, shaking my hand.

Without saying goodbye to anyone I left Kenley on August 4th and caught the first train from London to Digby. I'd never been more depressed in my life. As it was to turn out, the transfer to Chadburn's Wing was the best thing that could have happened.

CHAPTER IV

Operations Inspired by W/C Chad Chadburn

Pete was my companion when I arrived, dejected, at Digby on August 4th and I could not have had a better friend in time of need. Pete was a small brown and white dog of unusual intelligence and unfailing loyalty. He'd grown up in the Air Force and was completely habituated to the turbulence of dispersals and mess and the thundering of aircraft. Considering himself more a partner than a pet, he'd carry my gloves in his mouth to the kite, stand on top of the bay to watch our take-offs, and return to his post when he heard, long before anyone else, the deep tones of the Wing returning to base. He loved to go with me on my lap when I taxied Spits to maintenance and would like to have done the same on shows. Pete was a real pal on whom I could always count for sympathy and understanding.

My spirits were uplifted when I reported to Wing Commander Chadburn in his office. He was young, good-looking, laid-back.

"Heard about your trouble at Kenley, Art," he said. "And I think you were given a rough deal. Welcome aboard!" He grinned and shook my hand.

The C/O of 416 Squadron, S/L Grant, equally warm in his greeting, introduced me to F/L Kelly Walker, O/C of A Flight, to which I was assigned. I sensed a certain reticence however in some of his senior pilots who may have seen me as a rival in their advancement. They needn't have worried as my sole aim was to put up a good show and redeem myself. Soon, once again just another F/O, I became an accepted member of the City of Oshawa Squadron and good humour replaced gloom when I discovered how lucky I was to be in Chad Chadburn's Wing.

Digby was not as impressive a base as Kenley but it had an atmosphere that was buoyant and exhilarating. Morale was high and the esprit de corps I sensed animated everyone. The Station Commander was Group Captain Ernie McNab DFC. Short and stocky and in his late thirties, Ernie had won his DFC as C/O of Number 1 Squadron, the first all-Canadian outfit to go on operations. He was quiet-spoken and modest with no side to him and the pilots felt he was one of them. Digby was a happy station and to Ernie went much of the credit.

But it was the vibrant personality of its Wing Commander that made Digby unique. It was felt by all—pilots, ground crew, support staff—and when the youthful, blond Wingco visited dispersals and hangers faces lit up. Chad had all the qualities of a natural leader, on the ground and in the air. The adjective "inspired" was more than apt as his leadership was effortless, stemming from character rather than conscious act. He was worshipped by his pilots. I sensed this as they crowded around him in the mess, beer in hand and "shooting the shit" as he would say, or at the Wing's favourite pub in Lincoln where he was always the centre of festivities. In his company laughter abounded.

Chad instilled confidence in all who flew with him. He was an excellent pilot and marksman and superb Wing leader. Steady and cool, he gave his orders calmly and nearly always with some quip that made you smile and relax.

"Don't panic, chaps," he'd say when forty-plus bandits were reported. "We'll just about make it I figure!" or, going too close to Dunkirk, "Get well into that flak, chaps!" Confronting a large gaggle of Huns, he cracked, "Okay, m'lads, we'll go through them like shit through a goose!"

In pre-mission briefings Chad was a showman, deliberately putting on an act to relieve tension, laughing and joking as if planning a picnic. Essential information on course, height, speed and tactics was given in colourful slang of his own coinage, some of it bawdy.

"We'll go thataway," he'd say, pointing to North Foreland on the map, "And we'll meet up with the big boys at North Foreskin." You always started engines on "tit-pressing time" and on taking off you "gave her the goose." His fame as an entertainer spread and many unauthorized personnel including WAAFS sneaked into his briefings and, his enthusiasm being contagious, after them his pilots headed for their kites full of beans.

An astute and generous tactician, Chad always sought to get as many as possible of his pilots into the action, the objective being to do maximum damage to the enemy rather than increase personal scores. There were only two squadrons in his Wing—402 and 406—but by the end of November, five months after its formation, it had destroyed forty-two enemy aircraft, probably destroyed and damaged many others, and had won six DFCs and one DFM. On August 22nd Chad, already holding a DFC and Bar to the DFC, was awarded the DSO, the citation reading in part "(he) has displayed exceptional leadership and great skill and his fine fighting spirit has set a most inspiring example."

On being banished to Digby I'd resigned myself bitterly to a quieter life in the air with little chance of encountering the enemy. This was 12 Group which, as I remembered from seventeen months earlier, was a backwater, squadrons returning here for rest and re-training. But I had not counted on Chadburn. When given the Wing in July he'd insisted that it be fully operational and Headquarters had agreed. Digby was no more than a home station and the Wing was operating from a dozen forward bases from Norfolk to Cornwall. No dead end this and I was delighted!

There were thirty-four wing shows in August, most of them ramrods escorting seventy-two or thirty-six Marauders on bombing attacks on marshalling yards, aerodromes and other targets in Holland and northern France. Being a newcomer, I was assigned to only fourteen, missing out on two in which the Wing mixed it up with the Hun. On a ramrod to Bernay on the 17th, 416 broke into ten or more Me 109s diving toward the bombers but in the dogfight my Number 2 was hit and I was ordered out of the fray to shepherd him home. For me real action started in September.

German fighters were becoming ever more aggressive, sometimes making co-ordinated attacks on bomber formations simultaneously from above and below. On a ramrod with Marauders to St. Pol on September 4th twenty Me 109s climbed to attack the first box of bombers. Chad, leading 416 on close escort with me as his Number 2, broke into them. He followed two in a sharp turn to starboard, firing as he did so and continuing in the turn. Almost on his tail, I gave a three-second burst at one of them and it burst into flames. Wheeling around to keep up with the Wingco, I fired at another who suddenly appeared in front and smoke poured from it. Chad reformed on the port of the Marauders with one section only, the other two having lost altitude in the melee. Coming up to rejoin they reported a gaggle of FW 190s diving down out of the sun. Chad broke toward them and fired at the leader head on. It exploded and plummeted down in pieces. The rest of the Huns got into a defensive circle below but scuttled away and disappeared when we went after them.

In a separate engagement, 402 Squadron, on rear cover, split up an attack by another pack of 109s and downed four of them. The total score of the Wing in the short battle was six destroyed and two damaged. No bombers were lost but 416 almost lost Dave Prentice, one of its veteran pilots. Shot up badly in the first dogfight, he'd been forced to bail out and had plunged into the sea a few miles off the French coast. Picked up by the courageous crew of an air-sea rescue float plane, he returned to base with nothing more serious than a sodden uniform.

There were eight shows in the following six days, all ramrods to aerodromes and marshalling yards in northern France. On a ramrod to Beaumont le Roger on the 10th good luck flew with me. Over Rouen on the return leg the oil pressure in my kite dropped to almost zero and the engine began to grumble. A dozen or more bandits were seen climbing to attack the last box of Marauders but changed their minds when 402 went after them. I was relieved as the engine packed up completely before we reached the English coast. Fortunately I was able to dead-stick into Friston, red flares warning other planes away. A fitter said something about a faulty connecting rod.

An embarrassing incident occurred on September 21st, recorded obliquely in the logbook, in mortifying detail in the diary, and always kept secret. It started when the Squadron was to take off from Manston to cover Marauders bombing the aerodrome at Beauvais and I had come as supernumerary with the spare kite. When the extra fuel tank on Green 4's Spit sprang a leak I was ordered to take his place. It was one of the few times I flew as "tail-end Johnny."

While the bombers were making their run-in Chad led the Wing further south to head off any Jerries who might attempt to have a go at stragglers. There were none but as we turned back to rejoin the Marauders I saw a solitary aircraft at six o'clock about 3,000 feet below. I reported it to S/L Kelly Walker who had replaced S/L Grant as C/O a couple of weeks earlier.

"Can't see it," Kelly replied. "But go and investigate if you like." With no Germans about the tail-end Johnny wouldn't be missed.

I broke away, dived toward the bogey, and as I got close saw it was an Me 109. He was tootling along serenely, straight and level, a sitting duck ready for the taking! Suddenly he saw me, turned on his back and went down. I followed in tight turns and whenever he appeared in the sights fired with cannon and machine guns, stupidly not realizing I was skidding, the bullets going wide of the mark. I fired and missed all the way down to the deck when the Hun, undoubtedly a mite scared, had to straighten out. Pushing the throttle through the gate I caught up and when he was a hundred yards away pressed the gun button. Nothing happened—I was out of ammunition!

At that point I went crazy. I was in his slipstream but got closer, thinking of chopping off his tailplane but at the last minute pulled up beside him. There were two tears in his port wing but otherwise he seemed to be untouched. He was looking at me and, completely off my head, I waved and yelled inanely, "Have a go at me!" He declined the invitation and, sanity returning, I pulled away and streaked home on the deck, cursing all the way.

At Manston I told the C/O that I'd shot at a Hun but missed, which was true, had used up the rest of the ammunition on ground targets, which was false, and I persuaded the fitter not to send the film to the debriefing. I wondered what the German, the other clot, had reported when he got home. The incident tormented me for days: my shooting had been disgraceful and my actions idiotic—probably the only time a Spitfire pilot had flown formation on a Messerschmitt over France. I was reminded ruefully of "P/O Prune," the ludicrous cartoon fighter pilot who committed all the blacks in the book and got away with it.

The Wing was now commuting from Digby to Herston, Tangmere and Coltishall. On September 22nd the usual force of seventy-two Marauders had a go at the fighter base at Evreux. Again the Jerries responded, 50-plus being reported in the target area. They were all FW 190s and Chad, leading 416, bounced some of them as they climbed toward us. Leading a section now, I chased four down to 3,000 feet, closed to 250 yards on the trailing one and fired a short burst, seeing flashes on the fuselage as he disappeared into clouds. Climbing to rejoin the Squadron we encountered another 190 coming down, his round nose getting bigger in seconds, and I got in a short head-on shot. He went right through the section, miraculously missing everyone, trailing a stream of smoke according to my Number 3.

As raids on aerodromes were provoking enemy reaction, operations ordered a third bombing of Beauvais on September 24th. Again Jerries were about and 416, on close escort, broke into some of them streaking down out of the sun. After the break we returned to the bombers but Chad, leading 402 above and behind, continued after them, destroying one while Mitchener, a Flight Commander, got another as a probable. I was thankful to get safely home as there was a sizeable hole in my tail unit, a lucky miss by one of the 190s who'd come through.

There were two shows on September 27th, both long ones. Briefed for the first at Wellingore near Digby, the Wing flew across the North Sea to Den Helder to rendezvous with and give cover to Fortresses returning from a raid on Emden. They'd clearly had a mauling from German fighters or flak as there were many stragglers. Their rear gunners must have been edgy but they'd learned aircraft identification and didn't fire at us when we got close. No Huns appearing, all the Forts managed to get safely home. After a quick lunch at Wellingore we flew south to Tangmere to escort Marauders bombing an aerodrome near Conches-en-Ouche. Near the target a dozen FW 190s came down from above but 416, on close cover, succeeded in breaking them up, firing and being fired upon in the process. Seeing the action, Chad with 402 followed the Jerries down and he and his boys destroyed one and damaged others. No bombers were lost.

It had been a busy period and we weren't unhappy when storms rolled in the next morning, grounding us at Tangmere for three days. Every evening, Chad in the lead, we assembled at the bar for more than the usual single mug of beer. Tangmere was a good station for socializing as it hosted many transient outfits like ours and its mess was a lively one. One night during our stay there was a gathering of well-known pilots of the Battle of Britain, all now senior officers. Their joking and reminiscing about yesteryear, their tales recounted in light-hearted understatement, were fascinating. The most jovial of them and obviously the most popular was a squadron leader whose face was horribly disfigured by fire.

The weather restricted flying considerably in October but on the 2nd the Wing, operating from Coltishall, was despatched on a "Jim Crow" sweep from Texel to Ijmuiden in Holland to divert German fighters from a bombing raid by Fortresses further south. None was diverted and we returned home frustrated. The following day we escorted Marauders on a successful raid on Schipol aerodrome, the huge German base near Amsterdam. The Coltishall Wing, providing high cover, broke up an attack of twenty-plus Me 109s and when some came through Chad, leading 416, fixed on a tail-end Johnny and fired a short burst. It broke apart and pieces splashed into the sea. In two minutes he had the Squadron back in position on the port side of the bombers.

When F/L MacDonald was tour-expired on October 4th I was named O/C of A Flight but confirmation was delayed presumably because Headquarters considered the punishment for low flying had not been long enough. Ernie McNab and Chad persisted and on the 19th I regained the lost stripe and was officially designated Flight Commander. I was mightily content particularly as the promotion was warmly greeted by A Flight pilots. Contentment was made complete when S/L Freddie Green, the old chief of 421, now back on his second tour, was given command of the Squadron. He was a character, a coiner of colourful expressions and a generator of esprit de corps. I was convinced that no Wing anywhere could possess a better triumvirate of leaders than the Digby Wing with Chad, Freddie and Geoff Northcott, C/O of 402.

Restless because of the continuing bad weather, all the pilots of 416 welcomed a diversion in mid-month when the Squadron was transferred to Ford in Sussex to join two squadrons of a Spit IX Wing for deck-landing exercises. They'd been organized by the Air Force and Navy in preparation for an eventual invasion of the continent, to determine whether Spitfires could land unassisted on the deck of a certain type of carrier. For the exercises the runway was shortened by markers to the length of the carrier and pilots were invited to land and stop within them. This required an approach near stalling speed and while some pilots succeeded others did not, many going past the markers and four stalling and crashing, damaging their kites but not themselves. Churchill came for the final demonstration on October 15th and we were pleased with our performance as only three Spits, all Mark IXs, crossed the markers and went into the theoretical sea beyond. But the findings must have been negative for while Spitfires continued to take off from carriers they never to my knowledge landed on them, at least not without assistance.

There were three ramrods and one roadstead in the last part of October, one in the foulest of weather, the return through fog being somewhat dicey. The Jerries didn't like the weather either as they stayed away from all four. On the last show, a ramrod of more than two hours' duration, the Wing was forced to land at Kenley where, as at Tangmere earlier, it became weather-bound, this time for six days. Many of my 421 pals were still there and I was vainly pleased to meet them with two stripes again on the shoulder. Expecting the weather to clear daily we remained on the station, regretfully missing out on a blow-up in London but making up for it by nightly parties in the mess.

The Wing's most successful single operation occurred on November 3rd. After early morning fog we took off at eleven and headed for Coltishall on the coast to join the Spit Wing there on Ramrod 290, another bombing raid on Schipol aerodrome in Holland. We were assigned to close escort of the seventy-two Marauders flying in four boxes of eighteen, the Coltishall Wing to high cover ahead of the bombers. It was a clear and cloudless day, ideal weather for bombing and for air fighting.

At two o'clock we rendezvoused with the big boys as they climbed over the North Sea. Chad, leading 402, took up position slightly above and to the right of the first two boxes while Freddie with 416 covered the last two, also on the right. Flak appeared at the Dutch coast where we dropped our extra fuel tanks. On the way into the target the flak intensified, the sky full of ugly black and grey blotches bracketing the bombers, but they plowed steadily on. Over Schipol the leading boxes released their bombs and, still in close formation, turned port and headed back toward the coast. You could see the explosions below, on the runway and buildings around it, right on the mark. When our boxes dropped their loads and started to turn we wheeled with them, north and then west, sticking in close.

German fighters arrived as the first bombers reached the coast and we heard Chad order 402 to get into them. Apparently twenty 109s had attacked without being aware there were Spits about. In the dogfights that followed Chad and

Mitchener destroyed two each and Northcott got one. Two of the Huns bailed out, one—the first of Mitch's victories—before his aircraft had been hit.

416 was on the starboard of the last box of Marauders, my section closest. Looking behind and above them I saw a gaggle of Huns diving down toward the bombers. Reporting to Freddie, I broke left and to disperse them gave a short head-on burst at the leader. The gaggle split, one group going left, one right. Following those on the right I got in a two-second shot on the trailing one and smoke poured from it. As more Jerries were coming down I called a break to starboard and completing the turn caught a glimpse of a Spit chasing a 109 straight down, the Spit losing glycol. Suddenly there was another 109 in front of me, less than a hundred yards away. I fired, saw flashes on his wing root, and was just about to finish him off when my guns jammed! As I turned away the 109 exploded, hit a second time by Danny Noonan, my Number 3. The rest of the Squadron got into the action, Doug Booth downing one and Danny getting a second lower down.

When Freddie ordered the Squadron to reform I was pleased to do so, having no guns. It was only when we were back in position on the starboard of the bombers that I realized my Number 2, Jacobs, was missing. It must have been his kite I'd seen going down and streaming glycol.

The battle seemed to have lasted seconds but in fact almost ten minutes had elapsed between the first sighting of Huns by Chad and our re-grouping off the coast. In this short period the Wing shot down nine German fighters and damaged others, this total in a single combat being a record by Canadians at the time. Sadly, one Marauder with its crew was lost and several other crew members in damaged bombers wounded.

We celebrated our victory that night, hoisting one as was the custom for those we'd lost, the bomber crew and my Number 2. I was shaken by the loss of Jacobs, blaming myself for not calling the break sooner. This had been the young lad's first operational flight and I'd taken him as my Number 2 thinking he would be safest tucked in behind me. I wrote to his parents expressing the hope that he'd landed safely and been taken prisoner. Sometime later we learned he'd crashed and been killed.

You daren't linger thinking about losses: you had to forget and go on. Forgetfulness came most easily at the bar, watery beer in hand, as laughter was an amnesiac and togetherness the cement of good morale. When the Wing was grounded by bad weather reunions at the bar lasted longer and the foot marks on the mess ceiling testified to their hilarity. Nothing erased thoughts and lifted spirits more than a good blow-out.

In the week following the Wing escorted Marauders on three bombing attacks on German fortifications at Cap Griz-Nez and one on a similar target near Cherbourg. No Jerries interfered but the flak was heavy and most unfriendly. There was also a race on an aerodrome near Lille but the 10/10th cloud kept the enemy away and the Marauders dropped their bombs by dead reckoning.

On November 13th I led a section of four on a rhubarb into Holland, a mission that could have been my last. The Dutch underground had reported that the German torpedo bombers harassing Allied shipping were doing their training over the Zuider Zee and I thought it might be possible, in the right weather, to sneak across the eighteen-mile stretch of land between the coast and the practicing area and have a go at them before the Germans realized what was happening. Chad and

Freddie were lukewarm about the idea but when Intelligence conceded there was better than a fifty percent chance of success they reluctantly agreed to let me go. Chad insisted, however, that I take a second section of four to Coltishall, the jumping off base, to be on hand if support were needed on the way back.

I waited for the best weather—cloud over Holland low enough to nip into if attacked in force by Hun fighters but high enough so as not to prohibit practice flying by the bombers. I studied intelligence reports and supporting maps of gun positions along the coast and inland and got a profile chart of the coastline showing church steeples, buildings and other high structures between Den Helder and Haarlem finally deciding on entry at a point just north of Ijmuiden. This should take us over a reportedly lightly-defended area en route toward Edam on the Zuider Zee.

Good navigation was essential, as if we hit the coast just a bit north or south of the course we'd be greeted by hot metal from anti-aircraft batteries. But it was difficult to be precise when flying the hundred and thirty miles over the North Sea in winter. To avoid being picked up by German radar we'd be flying at wave-top level where winds could be variable, and the direction and force of the wind were major factors in selecting and maintaining a course. I worked out several based on winds of varying strength from the north-west, west and south-west, their usual direction at that time of the year.

On the 12th the Wing was grounded by bad weather and Met reported it should be ideal the following day—cloud covering all of northern Europe, its base 3,000 feet over Holland. The pilots in flight knew what I was planning and all wanted to go. I picked eight with the most experience: for my section, keen-as-mustard Dubnick as my Number 2, reliable Danny Noonan as Number 3 and second-in-command, Gould with him as Number 4, the reserve section led by Dave Prentice, 2 I.C. of A Flight. I worked out final courses, in and out, based on the latest wind estimates and got all pilots to jot them down. After breakfast the next morning we flew to Coltishall for refuelling and final briefing. The Met officer there provided new estimates of the wind, now 20 mph from the northwest, and I amended the courses accordingly, giving the new ones to all pilots. Danny also had a copy of the coastal profile in case he had to take over.

Our section took off at 10:00 hours. The other section would follow twenty minutes later, fly to within sight of the Dutch coast, orbit and wait for my call if we were attacked on the way out. Radio silence was to be maintained except by me when confronting the bombers or by others if Huns appeared and a break was called for. We flew at cruising speed just above the waves in wide line-abreast formation. Map and profile chart strapped to the knee, I concentrated on compass and airspeed indicator, vital instruments in holding to a steady course.

The weather was better and the cloud base higher than forecast when we saw the Dutch coast on the horizon but I decided to go on. I could make out higher land to the right of our line of flight, a long, low stretch to the left. Very quickly the silhouette became clearer, two towers or steeples and some high buildings taking shape on the right. Comparing them with the profile I was sure it was Ijmuiden: the wind had been stronger than predicted and we'd been pushed south. Dipping my wings twice, I turned port thirty degrees and the others turned with me. After a minute I returned to the original course, allowing five degrees for the stronger wind.

The coast was about three miles away when I dropped the extra fuel tank, the rest of the section following suit. This being the signal for more speed, I pushed the throttle to the gate. There was nothing ahead but a long white beach with flat land beyond. As planned, I started to weave and we zoomed over the sand at fifty feet, pulling up a bit to go over a row of trees. All was going well: we were into Holland and on our way!

Suddenly there was an explosion, a thunderous boom, and I was thrown onto the stick. Knocked out momentarily, I straightened up and pulled the stick back. When I opened my eyes I could see nothing, the cockpit was full of smoke. Thinking of fire, I hauled the hood back and immediately the smoke cleared. I closed the hood. Apart from a pain in the back of the head I seemed to be intact, everything working. The engine was still going—bless the solid Merlin!—and the kite still flying. I checked the instrument panel: RPM and oil pressure gauges okay, other engine instruments as well, but the airspeed indicator was at zero, turn and bank fluttering, altimetre wonky. The compass seemed to be alright and flying controls responded but there was a whizzing sound of air blowing into the cockpit.

I switched on the RT to call Danny, now close on my right. There was a dull sound in my ears and he didn't reply. I tried again but got only silence. The radio was dead and I realized I couldn't go on, couldn't lead without it. Danny was almost in formation now and Dubnick had come up on the port. I pointed to Danny and then ahead, trying to signal he should lead and go on with the show. He shook his head back and forth and pointed to my kite.

Tipping my wings, slightly as I didn't dare do more, I made a slow turn to starboard to get on the reverse, the homeward course. The other three turned with me. Danny took the lead and when I formed up on him I saw flashes from guns behind us. When well clear of the coast we started a slow climb to about 2,000 feet, Danny undoubtedly thinking I might need to have recourse to the parachute. Later he told me he'd ordered the reserve section to return to base.

I was mightily relieved to see the coast of Norfolk as bailing out into the North Sea in winter was hardly a cheerful prospect. Danny led me down to the runway at Coltishall and it was only after getting out of the plane that I realized how lucky I'd been. A 20 mm shell had blown a huge hole in the fuselage on the left, exploded inside and come out in a hundred pieces on the right, shattering the perspex behind my head. The armour plating had protected me from the shrapnel scattered round inside the cockpit.

In retrospect I conceded that Chad and Freddie had been right about it being a risky operation though I still felt that had it not been for the fluke shot we might have pulled it off. The point of greatest danger had been when crossing the coast and here Intelligence had not been well informed about the density of coastal batteries. Even unsettled areas were heavily defended. It was true however that rhubarbs in general were not very productive. Ten days later Dubnick led Carpenter on a rhubarb to the Oosterschelde Estuary and while they destroyed a couple of locomotives Carpenter was shot down, wounded and taken prisoner.

On November 23rd we were again over the North Sea, this time at 10,000 feet and at Wing force. A German convoy protected by warships had been reported sailing off the Dutch coast and two squadrons of Beaufighters were despatched to attack it with cannon and bombs. The Digby and Coltishall Wings were sent out separately to prevent German fighters from intercepting the low-flying Beaus. On the first try in the morning there was low cloud and they failed to locate the ships but in the afternoon they found them and through heavy anti-aircraft fire sank one and put several others out of commission. But the intrepid pilots paid a heavy price as four of their planes were shot into the sea by the escorting warships. Above the action, we searched the sky in vain for the enemy though the Coltishall Wing, coming onto the scene after our departure, ran into a mass of Me 109s and destroyed four of them.

On the 26th I had another encounter with a Hun at deck level over France, this one with a tragic rather than a comic ending. We were on Ramrod 339, a bombing raid by Marauders on an air base near Cambrai and on the return leg I saw four aircraft taking off from a small airfield below and behind. I reported them to Freddie and he agreed my section could have a go, saying he'd cover us with the rest of the Squadron.

We turned and dived, throttle through the gate, everyone close, catching glimpses of the Huns below the low scattered clouds. When we levelled out we saw they were FW 190s, three in formation flying toward a cloud and a straggler some distance behind. We got on the deck below him, Dubnick in tight on my port, and caught up fast. Keeping the 190 squarely in the sights I concentrated on the trim to keep from skidding and when he was fifty yards away fired with cannon and machine gun. It exploded, pieces going in every direction and the fuselage bouncing in flames over a railway embankment. I broke right to avoid the muck but Dubnick, much too close, went right through it.

He called, "I've been hit, lost my prop I think!"

I urged him to climb and bail out but he came back calmly.

"No, I'll try to put her down."

There was a forest ahead and apparently thinking he wouldn't get over it he put the nose down. Going too fast he crashed in a cloud of dust, lost a wing and almost cart-wheeled over. I circled around but he didn't get out. We learned later he'd been killed on impact.

The other Huns had vanished into cloud and Freddie, above with the rest of the Squadron and seeing the action, called, "Okay, Green 1, reform and we'll get back to the big boys." We caught up to them as they were crossing the French coast.

The chase had been exciting but it left me completely dejected. I'd lost another Number 2, the second in three weeks, and saying it wasn't my fault didn't help. I downed several whiskies that night, again seeking forgetfulness. It came too quickly and I realized I was becoming callous, wanting to lead the boys as best I could but not wanting to think of them as individuals.

The day following there was another ramrod with Marauders, this time to Cherbourg, the Wing taking off from West Malling, but because of 10/10ths cloud the operation was eventually aborted. It was remembered however because of an amusing black committed by a new pilot in 402, Wally O'Hagan. When the Wing was climbing through cloud to rendezvous with the bombers Wally lost his place in the formation. He dived to below cloud level, saw an aerodrome nearby and, thinking he was still over England, lowered his wheels and entered the circuit. When his approach was greeted by unfriendly bullets he realized he was landing at a German base. Hauling up his wheels he skedaddled away, miraculously escaping from the surprised and erratic gunners below.

I missed the last show in November, stepping aside to let Freddie take the flight when Chad took the Squadron. Over Abbeville 402 the Squadron was pounced from out of the sun and Art Coles was shot down and taken prisoner while Dean MacDonald, also hit, was trapped in the cockpit and went straight in. All the Huns got away.

Winter weather came to stay in early December and there were only a few shows, all of them uneventful. On the 19th, in part because of the weather, the Wing was posted for a fortnight to the armaments practice camp at Peterhead on the east coast of Scotland north of Aberdeen. Another reason for the move seemed obvious: the Wing had been operating actively for six months and its pilots were in need of a short break. A third reason was assumed: Headquarters wanted to quarantine the wild Canadians in an isolated spot over the partying Christmas period.

We lived up to our notorious reputation and subjected the staid RAF personnel of "Peterheed'"to a series of boisterous celebrations they would long remember. The weather co-operated by limiting the number of gunnery practices and every night there were thrashes in the mess with much merriment and many harmless blacks. On Christmas there was a day-long party for all ranks and on New Year's Eve—Hogmanay—Chad led the Wing by private buses to Aberdeen there to join scores of friendly Scots in joyous first-footing along the blacked-out but festive streets of that lovely city. Some pilots had flasks but there was no need for them as at every door you were welcomed in and given a nip. There was singing and laughter for hours but no one became drunk, the dancing and cold temperatures keeping everyone sober, relatively speaking.

Before leaving Peterhead the Wing received a cable announcing that Chad had been awarded a Bar to his DSO. The citation read: "This officer has displayed outstanding leadership, great tactical skill, and courage. Since being awarded the

Distinguished Service Order he has led his formation on a large number of sorties during which twenty-three enemy aircraft have been destroyed and many others damaged. Wing Commander Chadburn shot down six of this total himself. Much of the great success achieved during this period can be attributed to this officer's sterling qualities." This gave excuse, though none was needed, for a riotous farewell party.

After dinner on January 6th Chad took me aside and suggested I might be ready for a rest. I protested but he grinned and said, "You've had a pretty good go, Art." The next day Freddie said nothing but I sensed from his look that I'd soon be getting the chop. Pete sensed it too as for the first time he followed my kite out of the bay and the poor little pooch was blown over backwards by the slipstream. We were flying to Tangmere for yet another ramrod to Cherbourg, and I hoped there'd be Huns on what might be my last show. But it was not to be: the weather was foul and the Huns didn't oblige.

We were grounded the following day. As I got out of the Spit after testing its cannons, Freddie came up, punched me in the stomach and said laconically, "You can take your parachute to Stores, Chum, as you won't be needing it again for a while." I'd been on operations for twenty months, had put in more than the usual number of hours for a tour, and I admitted to myself I was a mite tired. There was a party that night after which, I was told later, the boys put me to bed.

After a week of leave I was posted as Operations Officer to 22 Wing, a new Canadian formation of three Spitfire and three Typhoon squadrons and served first with 143 Airfield at Ayr and Digby and then with 144 Airfield at Westhampnett. At the outset the work was interesting—the organizing of operational exercises and planning tactics—but it was theoretical and repetitive and soon I became restless. I had needed a rest but three months of it was demoralizing and I yearned to be back on ops. To get into the air I borrowed kites whenever I could— Spitfires, Hurricanes, Austers and a Typhoon. In March I flew a Hurricane to Kenley for a 416 party and while there pleaded with Chad, also on rest, to use his influence in getting me back to a squadron, and in April, again with a Hurricane, I went to Tangmere to press my case with the C/O of 421. I pestered Headquarters by letter and phone, so much that they eventually posted me on a one-month repatriation leave to Canada. I arrived in B.C. on June 4th, one day before the invasion of the continent, and while I was pleased to be home the timing of the leave could not have been worse. Well before the month was up I wanted to be back.

Chad Chadburn and Freddy Green, both ham actors.

B.26, Normandy. 403 pilots outside their tent with photo of a friend.

Sunday near Evereux. Popular Padre Scott always drew a crowd of sinners.

W/C Johnnie Johnson and S/L Wally McLeod after a sweep around Paris.

Squadron 443, The Hornets. Art Sager center, Blades and Fuller either side.

B.82, Graves, Airmen's Mess, Squadron Bash. Showing how to do it.

For most it was the first time ever.

Beginning to discover it was stronger than ginger ale!

My rigger and fitter, York and Smitty, to whom I owed my life.

Sweet Nelly Van der Aa, 21. She and her family adopted 443.

Spitfire XVI S/N TB476, my "Ladykiller." B.90, Petit Brogel.

Beating up flying control with Charlesworth, Art Sager in clipped wing version.

B.90, lining up for take-off.

Chocolate for eggs. Stevenson and Collins bargaining in Flemish.

Directing a skit in "Hash and Ham."

A priest offers free lessons in German.

"R" Day. The beginning of the air armada crossing the Rhine.

CHAPTER V

Harassing the Wehrmacht Back Into Germany

C anada was a long way from the war in distance and outlook and I felt out of place. It was pleasant being with loved ones but the news of air battles over the beachhead pressed on my conscience. When the report came through of Chad Chadburn's death in an air collision, I was desolated and determined to get back on operations as quickly as possible. But it was not until July 14th at Dorval that I was able to hitch a ride to England on a Liberator and not until August 6th that I wangled a posting to 403 Squadron in 127 Wing at B.2 near Bayeux in Normandy.

127 Wing comprised four squadrons—403, 416, 421 and 443—and was led by Wing Commander Johnnie Johnson, "Iron Bill" McBrien being the Group Captain. B.2, once pasture land, had been bulldozed flat and its runway covered with heavy metallic mesh that produced roars on take-offs and landings. Flying Control, Operations, Intelligence and Administration

operated from trailers while everything else was under canvas: you slept in tents and ate in tents, the food basic compo rations supplemented by eggs and corn bought from local farmers and cooked in pots on open fires.

British and Canadian armies under Montgomery were driving along the coast, having broken through the Panzer Divisions blocking them around Caen, while the Americans under Bradley and Patton were rooting the Germans out of the Cherbourg Peninsula, Patton making a high-speed sweep west and south to clear them from Brittany. Hounded on two fronts, the Huns were retreating eastward. Their tanks, troop carriers, armoured vehicles and guns, some hauled by horses, crammed the roads and lanes between Honfleur and Evreux on the east and between Vire, Falaise and Argentan on the south, this lethal escape route becoming known as "The Falaise Gap." The Germans moved mostly at night and, camouflaged, holed up in woods and orchards during the day. Our task was to delay their retreat by doing the maximum damage to their transport and armour. Spitfires had become ground attack aircraft and our sorties "armed reccos," some with bombs slung under the fuselage.

I was introduced to this new kind of fighting by flying as Number 2 to the Flight Commander and quickly gained experience by leading sections of two or four. Intelligence gave the area to be covered with the current bomb line and, cruising at 5,000 to 8,000 feet, you searched roads and byways between map coordinates. When the enemy was sighted—a flash of metal, a sudden movement, grey-green forms under trees—you dived one after the other into the attack, dropping your bomb if you carried one on the first pass and following up with cannon and machine gun. Hopeless in deflection shooting, I was a bit more accurate in bombing and firing on sitting targets and in the first two weeks amassed a creditable score of "flamers," "smokers" and "damaged." Not included in this total were three poor horses harnessed to guns and a fake ambulance with Red Cross markings I didn't attack but from which a dozen soldiers emerged firing rifles and machine guns.

It was a necessary job but not a pleasant one. The hunting for targets and quick planning of attacks were exciting but the strafing of despatch riders and soldiers in lorries turned the stomach, though less so when dropping bombs on tanks and shooting up armoured vehicles and mobile guns. When attacked the Germans responded with heavy anti-aircraft fire against which the soft-bellied Spitfire had no protection. Beating up ground targets was no piece of cake; in those two weeks three pilots were lost and many, some wounded, returned with damaged kites. In view of the odds, armed reccos were verboten for the Wing Commander, the continuation of his leadership being much more important than the destruction of MT.

It was a relief to be despatched on two high front-line patrols. On the first, on the 18th of August, I was leading a section of six when, at 15,000 feet over Dreux, Control gave us a perfect interception onto a squadron of American Thunderbolts, while on the second we were vectored in a futile chase of bogeys over Versailles, missing out on a mass of forty Huns encountered by another squadron. But how good it was to be flying above the slaughter on the ground with only Messerschmitts and Focke Wulfs to contend with!

In the warm and mostly sunny days of mid-August we flew two or three times a day and were frequently on readiness at the end of the strip. However, as pilots outnumbered serviceable aircraft, there were several periods when we were not on the roster. Sometimes on these occasions we hitch-hiked rides on army lorries to Bayeux for shopping or into Caen to see the havoc war had wrought. The city had been almost completely devastated, largely by bombing, and we were greeted coldly by Canadian and Polish soldiers patrolling in the rubble. They were not well disposed to men in blue as a week or so earlier, by some monumental error, they had been bombed by Fortresses and hundreds of their fellows had been killed and wounded. Had we not convinced them we were fighter pilots we could have been shot on the spot.

Because of the aircraft shortage four of us were sent by Anson to Bognor for replacements and on the lorry to B.21, the Anson airstrip further east, we had another opportunity of observing the legacy of all-out war. All along the route there were demolished villages, burnt-out vehicles and tanks, gouged roads and collapsed bridges, the countryside scarred by the tracks of tanks that had cut ruthlessly through gardens, fields and orchards. Everywhere there were hastily-dug graves marked by white crosses, Allied and German soldiers buried where they died.

At B.21 we boarded an old, crowded Anson and after a heavy take-off set course for England via Corridor 10. Fighter pilots hated flying in Ansons, hated flying as passengers in any plane for that matter. Brave "Brillcream" boys had no confidence in pilots of transport planes and when forced into them usually smuggled a mickey of whiskey aboard to calm the nerves. A verse was added to a popular ditty to describe their feelings:

An Anson was leaving the Normandy coast
Bound for Old Blighty's shore
Heavily laden with terrified men
Going back to the land they adore;
When down came a Messerschmitt 109F

And filled the old kite full of lead...

There'll be no promotion this side of the ocean

As all the poor bastards are dead!

One afternoon four of us not on roster accompanied the Wing Padre, Padre Scott, in his Bedford van to No. 7 Canadian Field Hospital west of Bayeux, there to visit pilots who had been wounded, some awaiting transfer to England. After touring the wards, the Padre distributing books and cigarettes, we were invited for tea with the nurses in their tents behind the hospital. We arrived at a propitious moment as several nurses were showering in a shoulder-high canvas enclosure nearby. It was enticing to catch glimpses of bare flesh and a unique pleasure to drink tea outdoors with attractive young ladies, some of whom were clothed only in white towels. The Padre, a popular character with a sense of humour, enjoyed the experience as much as we did, further strengthening his reputation as one of the better "Jesus Christ Liaison Officers."

In these hectic days of primitive living we missed the morale-boosting socializing over beer at the bar. Working long hours we were usually in our bunks by dark though often there were nightcaps around a fire and occasionally a movie in the mess tent. Once we were invited to a musical show on the grounds of the chateau at Creuilly, the site of Field Headquarters. Our enjoyment was limited however as we didn't see as much of the dancing girls as we would like to have seen, the Headquarters brass in the front rows blocking our view.

The German armies, battered but still intact, were now clear of the Falaise Gap and moving eastward fast on all fronts. To escape their pursuers they were now travelling into first light and during the day when there was low cloud to conceal their movement. On early and late patrols and diving through the cloud we found highways bumper to bumper with tanks, mobile guns, troop carriers and staff cars, ripe for the taking. Typhoons were better than Spitfires at the job but with practice we had become more efficient as well as more cautious, having learned to attack from different angles to disperse anti-aircraft fire. Hardened now to the dirty business, I added to my score of ground targets put out of action but would like to have had cleaner aerial ones. On the 23rd Johnnie Johnson led 421 and 443 Squadrons on a sweep around Paris, intercepted 50-plus Huns and downed twelve of them for the loss of three. Johnnie himself destroyed two, bringing his total score to thirty-seven.

The 23rd also marked the liberation of Paris and the radio reported "a delirium of happiness" among its inhabitants. The Free French Forces had been given the privilege of entering the city first, thus helping to restore French self-respect after four years of collaboration with the Nazis. In the minds of Air Force pilots this shameful collaboration was balanced by the courage of the French Resistance whose unsung heroes had risked their lives to hide pilots shot down and help them escape back to England.

For me the red letter day was the 24th when I was transferred to 416 Squadron and regained the post of O/C of A Flight. I was delighted to be back with the old gang again, an experienced and canny bunch of veterans who retained the gusto and good humour implanted by Chad and Freddie. S/L McIroy, DFC, who'd seen service in Malta, was now the C/O.

My first shows were two armed reccos over the lower Seine, attacking barges loaded with guns and the following day leading the Squadron, a first-light patrol in the Havre-Rouen area when the roads were bare of hostile traffic, the only victim being a speeding despatch rider. "Breaks in communication between German units save Allied lives" the instructions from Headquarters had said and this eased the conscience somewhat.

On the morning of August 26th Dave Harling led the Flight, encountered a mixture of Me 109s and FW 190s and with his fellows shot down three of them. In the afternoon I took the Flight on a show to protect Typhoons bombing bridges and the boys performed miracles in sticking with me as we whirled about chasing bogeys which turned out to be Thunderbolts. American fighters were frequently straying into our area, sometimes dropping silver paper to confuse the German radar. As it more often threw off our own the practice was soon stopped.

As B.2 was now too distant from the front line the Wing was ordered to move on the 28th to B.26, Illiers-l'Eveque, a former German base near Dreux that had been heavily bombed. When my Flight landed after the first morning patrol from B.2 we found the runway scarred with hurriedly-repaired bomb holes and were lucky not to have pranged, as four pilots of the Wing did later. A Flight was sent on three armed reccos, all of them successful, during the rest of that long day and, landing at dusk and tired, we were pleased to find that those who'd come in earlier had erected all the tents and furnished some of them with battered items from the rubble of the German mess. They'd also bought corn from a farmer and cognac and wine from a local "estaminet." As the lorries with the cooks and food had not yet arrived from B.2, that night under the stars we had a delicious corn feast amply spiced with liquid refreshment, during which the farmer, intrigued by our purchase of his corn, came to investigate. Shocked by the barbaric tastes of Canadians, he exclaimed "Mais le maïs, Messieurs, le maïs, c'est pour des animaux."

Fortunately for pilots who'd drunk too much wine the Wing was grounded by heavy rain for two days, giving all of us the chance to improve our living quarters and some an opportunity to visit Paris. On the 30th, borrowing the Wing Humber, I took six of the Flight to the liberated city, arriving at seven in the evening. Enthusiasm still reigned and along the route we'd been stopped several times to receive flowers, bottles of wine and kisses on the cheek from both sexes. After driving around goggle-eyed down the Champs Elysees, across the Seine to Les Invalides and the Tour Eiffel, we got rooms in the Hotel Splendid near the Arc de Triomphe, had an unbelievable meal, and then walked and talked to Parisians until midnight, two staying up later to "chercher les filles." After breakfast those of us who'd recovered walked to the Arc de Triomphe where we inspected, more closely than the monument, the scores of pretty girls going to work on bicycles, their lower limbs delightfully exposed by the breeze. Recovering the Humber and those who'd slept in, we left the beautiful city at nine, stopping to watch French soldiers flushing out suspected German snipers on the top floor of a building on our route.

By the first of September the American army was in Sedan, the British in Amiens and the Canadians east of Dieppe. German forces were reported moving in the open along the whole front and the Wing was ordered to attack those near St. Pol west of Arras. It was mid-afternoon and time for two sorties only, 421 going first and 416 an hour later. The C/O being still in Paris I was again leading the Squadron. After taking off I called S/L Prest, C/O of 421, now on his return leg.

"Weather's good but there's a helluva lot of flak," he reported.

Before five minutes were up three of my twelve pilots had turned back, reporting engine or instrument trouble.

We saw the flak as we approached St. Pol at 7,000 feet, the sky full of ugly blotches ahead and below us. I dropped the extra fuel tank and signalled the others to do the same. To confuse the German gunners we'd agreed to split up in singles and choose our own targets but before picking mine I ordered the Squadron to reform at the same altitude south of the town when I called in about twenty minutes.

It was hazy but you could tell there was traffic and armour below as gunfire was coming from all directions. Deciding to search a road and railway line north-west of St. Pol, I flew beyond the flak, turned back, dived and screamed on the deck into a valley leading into the town. Seeing movement ahead, I pulled up to 200 feet, then put the nose down and sprayed everything on the road—mobile guns, lorries, soldiers diving for cover. As I passed a gun opened up on the left from what looked like a haystack beside a string of railway cars. Twisting and skidding, I climbed back to 7,000 feet where, irrationally angry at the gun in the haystack, I decided to make a second pass and try to get it. This time I went down more slowly, hit the mobile guns and lorries a second time and, turning fast, hammered the haystack with everything. The gun was firing but it stopped abruptly.

Above at the rendezvous point some of the boys were milling about looking for new targets. By their joking natter on R/T I knew that all had carried out attacks: three were diving onto MT at a crossroads, some of which was already burning. Spotting horse-drawn guns on a road going toward Arras, I skidded down, steep-turned into them and let go with the rest of my ammunition.

It was now eight-fifteen and time to pack it up. I called the boys to reform and was relieved to see that no one had been clobbered. We returned to base just before dark. It was a successful do and while pleased with the performance of the nine who'd remained with me, I was disturbed by the reasons given by those who'd turned back. Investigating, I found that one was genuine, the other two dubious. Both pilots were new, and wanting to nip their twitch in the bud, I spoke to them over beer that night about the need for solidarity. They took it very well.

This armed recco was the last wing operation for three weeks. After only five days at Illiers the front line was again beyond reach and on September 2nd the Wing was declared non-operational.

Among fighter pilots nothing did more damage to morale than inactivity. Practice flying was limited because of restrictions on the use of petrol, visits to Paris rationed for the same reason, Ensa concerts and movies cancelled presumably because a non-operational outfit needed no such diversions. Flight Commanders organized games of football and touch rugby and some of us led groups of pilots on route marches for both the exercise and the wine in village cafés. But low spirits persisted and idleness provoked friction and an ugly kind of moodiness. What was needed was an all-out thrash and, the C/O being in Paris, I organized two of them, again with corn, cognac and plonk, and some good cheer was restored.

The ground crew, no longer under pressure, were also restless and down in the mouth, and so with the cooperation of the Padre we helped to improve their quarters and set up a party for them. One of the tasks of a Flight Commander and his 2 I.C. was the censoring, by eliminating military references, of the letters written by the "erks" and this provided insights into their feelings. Most letters revealed a certain loneliness, a need to preserve links with family and friends and a deep desire to be remembered by someone special.

On the sixth of September, again borrowing a wing vehicle, I took another group of pilots to Paris. The Padre had said "I went, I saw, and I was conquered" and everyone wanted to share the experience. We toured the sights, had a delicious meal, went to a show at the Lido and while there encountered a young French doctor who led us to a high-class house of ill-repute whose health standards he personally guaranteed. While most of us were content to talk to the beautiful, lightly-clad hostesses others disappeared to taste their inviting wares.

The battle for France was now over and the battle for Germany beginning. By September 13th the 7th American Army had crossed the frontier in two places and the British were at the Albert Canal in Holland. I was convinced that the final onslaught would be a holocaust as Hitler's fanatic creed demanded a grand Wagnerian climax of destruction. He'd revealed his malicious intent by the buzz bomb attacks on civilians in London where one thousand people had been killed and three thousand wounded.

On the 14th I flew to England for a new gyro sight and while there had two days of leave in London. I visited my landlady, Mrs. Hook, went to the Windmill Theatre with Bob Cook who'd recently escaped from France, had drinks at the Crackers and Wellington Clubs and spent a quiet evening at Mrs. Hancock's. Warm-hearted and generous, Mrs. Hancock was the adoptive mother of scores of Canadian fighter pilots who throughout the war found relaxation at her hospitable home in the country and at her Air Officers' Leave Club in London.

When I returned to B.26 morale was still at a low level. There was practically no flying, visits to Paris were prohibited and enthusiasm for rugby and other activities had waned.

Montgomery's paratroopers were now landing at Arnhem, the Americans fighting at Aachen, and being out of the action depressed everyone. To cheer ourselves up we lingered long over campfires at night, the veterans reminiscing about the past and re-telling stories about inimitable Chad Chadburn, memories of whom still sustained us. As one of the old hands remarked with pride and humility, "All who served under Chad retain a bit of him inside them and that's why we're still a good squadron."

Spirits soared when word finally came through of a move—to B.68 at Le Culot near Brussels. At dawn on the 21st S/L Prest, C/O of 421 and Acting Wing Commander, took off with all serviceable aircraft in his squadron and I followed with sixteen of ours. Johnnie Johnson and the C/Os of 403 and 443, delayed in Paris, got airborne in the afternoon.

B.68 was potted with bomb holes gravelled over and, while the runway was not as dangerous as the one at Illiers had first been, our landings stirred up clouds of dust. Most of the buildings on this former German base had been damaged by bombing and were under repair. 416 was assigned to a thick-walled barracks with holes in the roof where for the first night we were issued with two blankets each and invited to sleep on the floor. Famished by noon, we prevailed upon the cook, whose facilities had not yet arrived, to let us raid his stores and fill up on canned fish and canned beans. After these modest rations some of us commandeered a lorry and drove to the nearest bar to sample Belgian beer, reputedly better than the French. Our first impressions of Belgian civilians was not favourable as they seemed almost surly, but we forgave them as those near the aerodrome at least were obviously fed up with men in uniform, any uniform.

Disdaining the hard floor, I slept that first night in the dispersal hut, sharing the chairs with Slim, the corporal in charge. The next day the convoy from B.26 arrived with bunks, bedrolls and baggage and we were able to make ourselves reasonably comfortable in spite of leaks from the ceiling. While the ground crew's quarters were drier than ours they were forced to queue for meals in the rain and I arranged for the erection of tarpaulins to cover them. I'd been named Acting C/O though in practice shared the responsibility with Pat Patterson, O/C of B Flight. Pat, quiet-spoken and imperturbable, was an intrepid leader and a good pal.

The work assigned to us was much to our liking—patrols along the front line to search and destroy the Hun in the air. Allied troops had made airborne assaults at Nijmegen and Graves while the First British Airborne Division was fighting for survival at Arnhem. The Wing's task was to protect these forces from attacks by German fighters and fighter-bombers which, to avoid our radar, were flying at low altitudes.

Our first show from B.68 was almost a disaster for which I accepted some but not all of the blame. We'd been ordered to patrol at 12,000 feet between Nijmegen and Venlo and after flying for thirty minutes and seeing nothing were vectored east after bogeys that revealed themselves as other Spits. Disoriented above the 10/10ths cloud, I called Control for our position and a homing and it reported we were near Nijmegen and could let down to 5,000 feet. Had I timed our varying courses more carefully I'd have realized we'd been mistaken for another squadron as coming out of the cloud we were greeted by a massive barrage of flak from an industrial area on the Rhine. We climbed like dingbats back into the white stuff and were lucky to get away unscathed. On a second patrol that afternoon

I was able, after some searching, to get back to base without the help of Control though we landed after dark. Pat led the Squadron on a patrol the next day, uneventful except that four lost Spitfires of 126 Wing clung to us throughout. Map reading over the featureless part of Holland wasn't easy for newcomers to the area.

Now settled in, we decided to have a house-warming party. Good spirits prevailed but we wanted to initiate the new pilots who'd recently come on strength. Persuaded by the old hands when we were into our second beers, I gave a short talk on the traditions established by Chad, teamwork and the important roles of all members of the Squadron including Number 2s. Esprit de corps was not created by sermons but, adjudging from the reaction of the new boys, I felt I had learned something about instilling loyalty and confidence.

The last week of September was the busiest and most successful for the Wing in some time. It was also tiring as pilots were putting in two or three sorties a day and the Lutwaffe was coming up in numbers, fighting desperately to prevent the Allies from crossing the border. Patrols were usually at low altitude and those at 10,000 feet or above frequently ended up on the deck in pursuit of German fighters and fighter-bombers harassing the doomed paratroopers in Arnhem. In the last seven days of the month the Wing destroyed and damaged over twenty Me 109s and FW 190s. But there were losses as well, all of them grievous.

On the afternoon of the 25th the Squadron was vectored urgently to Arnhem where 50-plus Huns were reported. Flying just below the cloud we spotted ten 109s in tight formation below and we bounced them. Russel, leading the port section, cut the corner and got the tail end one with a burst in the cockpit. But it was a trap and the 109s were decoys as we were set upon by a mass of 190s diving through the clouds. I ordered a break and we turned into them, firing as we did so. Superior in numbers, the Huns elected to fight and we were forced into a series of defensive circles, trying to get one in our sights. Palmer and Fraser in the starboard section each reported hitting one while I fired three times, probably missing but in any case couldn't see much as I'd been hit somewhere and the Perspex was covered with a film of brown oil. In the middle of the dog-fight, the hottest I'd been in, Johnnie Johnson, leading 403 and hearing the natter, called for our position, saying he'd come to help. When he arrived the sky was clear of aircraft except for twelve Spitfires with sweating pilots aboard.

I was proud of the Squadron for sticking together through-out the five-minute battle. Our claim was three destroyed and one damaged, not bad for twelve against fifty, but Treleaven did not return, Cameron was shot up though he landed safely at Eindhoven and Dyke England was wounded. His Spit riddled with bullets, he made a magnificent crash landing at B.68. The two holes and broken oil line in my kite were quickly repaired.

There were three patrols for 416 on the 26th, all of two hours and more. Pat led the Squadron on the first one and after a fruit-less chase of an Me 262, the new German jet fighter-bomber, we were vectored to Nijmegen where again we spotted Huns on the deck, this time 190s, about forty of them in two formations. As my section of three was closest, Pat agreed we could lead the attack. Line abreast, McColl, Saunders and I dived toward the Huns in the second formation. For some reason they hadn't seen us and it was a perfect bounce. A hundred yards away I fired at a 190 directly in front. There were strikes all over its fuselage. It flicked left and kept going though I doubted it would do so for long. McColl and Saunders were firing at others at the same time and I saw one explode and the other go down in flames. As the rest of the 190s were no longer in sight we climbed to rejoin the Squadron.

But the Huns had not disappeared: they were ahead of us and we could see the rest of the boys milling about with them. When we got on the scene the dogfight was over and, concerned about petrol, I collected six of the Squadron and led them back to base. Two pilots in Pat's section arrived minutes later, reporting they'd lost their leader in the dogfight. Pat did not return. We learned later that he'd been hit, crash-landed and taken prisoner and that he'd lost an arm.

There were two more patrols for the Squadron that day on which we chased bogeys and were chased by flak and when we landed at dusk the boys, still shaken by the loss of Patterson, looked depressed and tired. Deciding a little smash was called for I piled the jeep with thirteen pilots and with Cuppy, Harling and McColl following on one motorbike we headed off on a pub crawl. Miraculously we returned to base intact, refreshed and in better spirits.

Our first patrol on the 27th was uneventful but the second brought results. East of Nijmegen, Harling, now my 2 I.C. and leading the port section, reported seeing Huns through a hole in the cloud, below and to his port. I ordered him to lead us down, saying we'd cover him. He needed cover as when we got through the cloud we saw a mass of 190s with bombs at deck level and an equal number of 109s as escort above them, at least fifty in all. Harling got a tag-end 109 right away and we went after the others who'd started turning to starboard. Suddenly I saw a 109 fifty yards away, fired and it exploded, parts going in every direction. Continuing in the turn I fired at another and it too exploded, losing its tail and a wing. We were now in a dog-fight in which it was hard to distinguish friend from foe. Seeing a Hun on my tail and firing, I broke in a stall turn to the right but knew he'd got me as I felt a jolt. Apparently I'd been hit in the tail unit as the controls were heavy and I couldn't stop the kite from climbing skywards. Ordering Harling to take over I headed slowly for base, fighting the controls all the way. I let down gradually, pushing, the stick forward as hard as I could and, cutting the engine in the approach to slow up, got the old kite reluctantly onto the ground.

I was relieved when all of the Squadron returned safely and pleased when they reported the joy. Harling had destroyed two Me 109s, Cuppy and Rainville one each and with my two this gave us a score of six destroyed, plus three damaged, with no losses. There was a tragic loss for 443 Squadron however. On a patrol in which Huns had been engaged its C/O, S/L Wally McLeod, DSO, DFC and Bar, was shot down and killed. A superb marksman, Wally had twenty-one destroyed to his cred-it and was the top scoring Canadian fighter pilot. His death was a sad blow.

The battle for Arnhem had now been lost, hundreds of para-troopers having been killed and the rest taken prisoner. At this point the front line was quiet and our patrols on the 28th were dull ones without even vectors onto bogeys. When we got back to base from the last one we found that our C/O, S/L McIroy, had returned and that Mitch Michener of 403 had been appointed O/C of Pat's flight. He led the Squadron on the sec-ond patrol on the 29th and did so with distinction. Near the Maas River the Squadron attacked a large formation of low-fly-ing Huns and destroyed seven of them without loss, Mitch get-ting two and increasing his total score to nine.

The weather was duff on September 30th when the Wing was ordered to move, in one hour's time, to its new base, B.82 at Grave in Holland. On landing we covered each other by sections as the field was close to the front and was frequently being attacked by Me 262s with anti-personnel bombs.

Harling led my flight on the first patrol while I remained to organize our dispersal facilities. I taxied an aircraft to maintenance and when I got out Group Captain McBrien was there, sitting in his jeep.

"Come along, I'll drive you back," he said. On the way he stopped at the briefing hall where all of the pilots of 443 Squadron were assembled. He walked in, ordering me to follow. In front of the group he said, "I'd like to introduce you to your new Commanding Officer, Squadron Leader Art Sager."

It was totally unexpected and I was floored. I'd hoped to get a squadron some time and had even dared to hope it would be 416 when the C/O finished his tour, but replacing Wally McLeod had never entered my head and the thought of stepping into his shoes left me feeling nauseated.

443 Squadron, later to be named "The Hornet Squadron," had been formed in Canada in 1942. After carrying out defensive patrols in Nova Scotia and Newfoundland it had been transferred overseas in January 1944 with S/L McLeod, DFC and Bar, as its Commanding Officer. It had joined 127 Wing, which after the invasion had moved to B.3 at St. Croix-sur-Mer in Normandy. The Squadron had established a fine record in air combat and ground attack and in recognition of his leadership its C/O had been awarded the DSO. I felt proud to have been selected as its second leader on operations.

CHAPTER VI

The Long Last Winter
and Final Assault

B.82, Grave, was an airfield on flat, boggy land beside the Maas River in eastern Holland near the German border, the most advanced air base in the British sector. We heard gunfire frequently and much too often. During the day Me 262 jets swooped down and dropped high-explosive bombs on buildings, aircraft and people. Our first task, requiring no persuasion to perform, was to dig slit trenches around the tented dispersals, and everyone carried a tin helmet. The pilots had been allotted cold but reasonably comfortable sleeping quarters in the town but the ground crew slept on damp ground in tents near the perimeter track. Ignoring the Wing Adjutant in whom I had little confidence, I authorized the Sergeant, Gordie Symonds, to send groups of his men into shattered villages nearby to search for oil stoves and lumber for the tent floors. Eventually 443's accommodation for its erks was the best in the Wing.

During the first week in command I led the Squadron on fourteen patrols and was delighted with the flying of my new team. On all the shows the pilots had stuck with me through thick cloud and in convoluted manoeuvres after bogeys and they displayed excellent air discipline without needless nattering. I had inherited two solid Flight Commanders in "Smokey" Stovel and Gordie Troke. There were a dozen or more veterans to back them up and the rest of the team seemed well above the average.

The patrols were shorter now, none exceeding an hour and a half, as in a few minutes after take-off we were over the front line. On two patrols we made futile attempts to shoot down 262 jet bombers, but had to concede the honour of getting the first one to 126 Wing. The first score for our Wing was made on March 5th when 403 Squadron bounced low flying Me 109s and got five destroyed and one probable.

On the 6th and 7th the RAF carried out a massive daylight bombing of German forces across the border east of Grave. On patrols later we saw the results: the Rhine blanketed with dirty smoke rising to 6,000 feet above Emmerich, Kleve and Bocholt, scores of buildings in these and other towns on fire. A pilot's fate would be uncertain were he forced to bail out over this area.

After landing from a patrol on the 6th we were returning to the billets in a lorry when a 262 roared down—you heard them only after they'd passed—and released a cluster of anti-personnel bombs on the aerodrome. We speeded back and found that most of the bombs had burst near a maintenance tent, killing three airmen. We helped as best we could in giving first aid to others who had been wounded.

All of the squadrons had constructed "anterooms" to add space and comfort to their dispersal tents. When ours was finished and furnished with purloined items including a boiler stove I decided a squadron thrash would be timely, a small one as we were on line for patrols the next day. From some undisclosed source "Bub" Fuller, a wily Maritimer, acquired several bottles of gin and lime juice and, acting as self-appointed barman, proceeded to lose track of which was which, thus adding to the general merriment. In the middle of the party I dragged out the usual homily on teamwork and then brought up the subject of the ground crew. The Group Captain had agreed that they could be granted seven days' leave in groups starting on October 15th and I suggested we help them financially. By unanimous vote the pilots agreed that the Squadron Fund, maintained by monthly assessment, should be used in its entirety to supplement the resources of erks going on leave. F/O Paul Piche, who had relatives in Belgium, said that he could obtain inexpensive bed and breakfast accommodation for them in Brussels and so, two days later and with the Groupie's permission, I sent him off in the Austen to complete the deal. Art Horral went with him to pick up a new Spitfire in Antwerp.

On an afternoon when the Wing was grounded by torrential rain four of us drove in the jeep to Nijmegen to scrounge for a better stove for the dispersal and to buy if possible a second-hand car for the Squadron. Stopping to ask questions and search in the rubble, we snaked our way through battered Nijmegen and then drove north across the Waal on a pontoon bridge to the town of Elst which presented a pitiful sight, its ruined houses revealing inner secrets: plates and cutlery still on kitchen tables, dolls on children's beds, clothes hanging in open cupboards—all the intimacies of domestic life brutally exposed when war had knocked on the door. Eventually we were halted at a roadblock by a cockney soldier. "Inybody on t'roads arter tis point, chum, 'll be shot no questions arsked!" he growled menacingly, rifle at the ready. We returned to Grave soaked to the skin with two old stoves found on a street, eight dead chickens from a farmer's yard, a box of apples and pears picked in an abandoned orchard, but no car. We also returned shocked by the calamitous effect of war on civilian life.

On October 12th, driving to the airfield for a four o'clock show, we got as far as the guard tent when we heard the zoom of a jet followed by explosions. Smoke and flames were rising from dispersals on the other side of the runway. As we tore across the field we saw Spitfires burning and heard their ammunition going off, and on arrival discovered that five of the airmen working on kites had been killed, twelve wounded, seven 443 and 416 Spitfires completely destroyed and ten badly damaged. No pilots had been killed though Chuck Charlesworth, hit in the arm by shrapnel, had to be taken to hospital. Moments after the attack, when bullets from burning aircraft were whizzing in every direction, Harling and McColl of 416 had courageously run out and taxied two Spits to a safer area.

It testified to the sang-froid of Sergeant Symonds and his men that we were able to get airborne with six aircraft on time. It was the usual patrol east of Nijmegen but for us it had only one objective: to find and shoot down any bloody 262 in the air. Control reported some were about and, sure enough, we saw two emerge from the clouds above and come hurtling down wide apart. We broke to try to get on the tail of the closest one but he was over five hundred yards away before I could fire. If curses carried bullets he'd have been a dead duck. So preoccupied had we been in searching the sky for jets, we were late in spotting two Me 109s strafing troops near Nijmegen. Without much hope we dived after them but they disappeared, leaving us with an urgent need to escape from the still-firing Allied gunners.

On the following day 443 and 403 Squadrons escorted a Dakota flying a "Mr. Smith" from Eindhoven to Brussels, a tricky show for 443 as, on close escort, we had to stay in formation close to stalling speed to keep at the slow pace of the Dakota. We learned later that our precious charge had been none other that King George VI who'd been visiting the troops in Holland. That afternoon there were more patrols and more bombs on the airfield, this time with only a few minor casualties.

Abruptly the mild and occasionally sunny days of fall gave way to cold and wet ones of an early winter, a consolation for the ground crew, as jets never bombed when there was low cloud. Because of the change in the weather and the scarcity of Huns in the air, the Wingco informed the C/Os that in future most shows would be armed reccos to harass the enemy on the ground. 443 would take off on the first one the next morning to the Bocholt-Borken-Wesel triangle, our targets MT, rail transport, barges and even civilian transport. When I told the pilots they weren't exactly enthralled though they knew we'd soon be back pretending to be dive-bombers. Most had had experience on armed reccos but these would be the first ones over Germany where the natives might not be particularly friendly. To buck them up I said that to maximize damage and minimize risks we'd use the same tactics that had proved successful over France—leaving decoys above to divert ground fire, attacking in singles, sneaking up on targets from different directions—but there was no doubt that a convincing demonstration would be good for morale.

Six of us got airborne at seven-thirty the next morning, crossed the Rhine at 8,000 feet and let down below scattered cloud over Bocholt. Seeing a train going out of the town, I told Green 1 to circle around with the rest of the boys while I had a go. I flew south, spiralled down to deck level, went back along the railway line and when I saw the train sprayed the boxcars and engine with cannons and machine guns. They stopped, the engine billowing smoke. As guns had started firing from Bocholt I didn't ask the others to follow and in any case this bit of derring-do was a demonstration only. There was another one on the way back to base when we spotted three lorries east of Emerich. Using the same sneak-up-on-them ploy, my Number 2 and I, going down separately, sent the lorries crashing into a ditch and a score of soldiers diving for cover. I was callous now; any German in uniform was the enemy even when running away. An hour after landing I took another six on a recco to Munster and on the return leg all of the section, singly, got into attacks on a railway engine with five carriages, a lorry with trailer and two troop carriers. We capped the day on a final recco in the afternoon by destroying two large tracked vehicles near Kleve. There'd been some ground fire on all three shows but because of our tactics it had been late and erratic. The demonstrations had succeeded and there was a lot of good cheer in the mess that night.

Worried about Piche and Horral who'd not returned from their dual mission in the Austen, I sent Fairfield in a Spit to check on their movements with Flying Control at Antwerp and Brussels. I was concerned mostly about their safety but also about the collapse of the housing arrangements for ground crew going on leave. In line with the decision taken a week earlier I gave each leave-taker a small grant from the Squadron Fund as well as a letter soliciting help in finding a bed and breakfast. The sergeant was sure they'd manage without reservations and certainly the twelve erks heading off to hitch-hike to Brussels didn't look at all concerned.

At regular intervals Group Captain McBrien convened meetings with the Wing Commander and the four C/Os and on the 16th the meeting in his office-tender concentrated on the question of operational hours. Two hundred hours was the generally accepted maximum for one tour but as a large number of pilots were close to this mark and as too rapid an exodus of experienced pilots could impair squadron efficiency, the Groupie announced that until further notice no more than two pilots of the Wing would be released each week. He pointed out that two hundred hours was not a mandatory limit and that pilots could be asked to put in much more. While agreeing, I argued for a flexible interpretation of the 200-hour practice, believing that some pilots took stress better than others and that keeping a man on after he'd become mentally fatigued could endanger his life unnecessarily and weaken the performance of the whole Squadron.

After the meeting I called the pilots together and informed them of the Group Captain's decision and the reasons for it. The 200-hour end of tour mark would no longer be observed and one should put hours out of one's mind; the war was a long way from being over, there was a lot of fighting ahead and absolute keenness was essential. Secretly I sympathized with some of the old hands who'd been on operations for a long time and concealed their tiredness. But orders were orders, and sometimes command could be a lonely place.

The weather closed in and it started to rain, heavily and continuously night and day. There was little flying as the airfield was only partly serviceable: in parts it was a bog, in other parts a lake. A big squadron blow-up was needed to lift the spirits of restless pilots and sodden ground crew. Earlier I'd asked the Groupie for permission to hold an all-ranks squadron party and he'd been most forthcoming. He suggested I drive to Group Headquarters in Eindhoven, see the catering officer there whom he'd phone in advance, and that I'd be able to get at least a hundred bottles of the excellent champagne Group had "acquired" from a hidden German supply. On the morning of the 17th Gordie Troke and I set off in the jeep to hunt for the liquid treasure.

At 83 Group Headquarters the Assistant Catering Officer said, "You're 127 Wing Bar Officer, I suppose?"

"Well, yes, yes, for the day only," I replied, mumbling the last words.

"Will you be taking the full allotment for the Wing?" he asked.

I nodded and he made out an order form for 275 bottles of champagne at 2,146 guilders which I signed, for the Wing to pay later; 443 would pay for those retained for the party. With the order we drove four miles south of the city to the A.O.C's mess, there to collect the precious loot from its huge "cave." Cunningham had his headquarters in the clubhouse of the golf course, his Fiesler Storch parked beside the 18th green, and the officers' mess was in the home of the president of the Phillips Company, a hundred yards away in the park-like woods beside the course.

When we'd piled the jeep high with cases held on securely with rope, I enquired politely if it would be possible to have a bite to eat before starting on the long journey back to Grave. The junior officer went to ask and returned. "I'm very sorry," he said. "The PMC says it's not possible as he has too many visitors and not enough food. He extends his sincere apologies." Driving home famished we ironized about the poor PMC, having difficulty feeding the hard-working staff of Group who lived in hazardous conditions near, well, fairly near the front line!

Sad news awaited us on our return to B.82. Fairfield, back from his search for Piche and Horral, reported that they'd checked in at Antwerp but apparently as Horral's Spit wasn't ready they'd taken off in the Austen the next morning without formally logging out. As they hadn't arrived at Brussels the only conclusion was that they'd been shot down en route. The

Adjutant issued a casualty signal while I sadly submitted an application for two replacements.

Met continued to promise it would be better tomorrow but with heavy rain still pouring down we were sure it was a tomorrow that would never come. All the roads were ankle deep in mud, passable only with four-wheel drive vehicles and in places not at all. The airfield, unsafe even for taxiing, was finally declared unserviceable. A change of base was clearly imminent, the leave of poor airmen was cancelled, and morale was low.

No squadron party could have been better timed than 443's on October 20th. I'd spent hours lining up entertainment—there was a lot of talent in our ground crew—and had issued a formal invitation: "The Officers and Airmen of No. 443 Squadron and No. 6443 Servicing Echelon request the pleasure of your company at a Squadron Thrash in the Airmen's Mess Tent on Tuesday, October 20th, 1944. Tits will be pressed at 20:30 hours and an indirect course will be flown after takeoff. It is hoped that all will get into the action and that the mission will prove successful."

The turnout was one hundred percent, pilots and erks in battle dress and gumboots, many wearing helmets against the rain dribbling through the tent, all carrying mugs. Free beer was served as a primer and then five pilots known for their relative sobriety handed out bottles of champagne still wrapped in fancy paper in return for an eight guilder ticket bought earlier. Cork-pulling time was 9:15 p.m. before which I demonstrated, with amazingly good luck, how to do it with minimum loss of the precious liquid.

The popping of corks sounded like gunfire. Then there was silence as the men started to drink from their mugs or straight from the bottle. Most had never tasted champagne before and you could feel their initial disappointment as they took large gulps and found this nectar of the Gods no stronger than ginger ale. Then, all of a sudden as the alcohol took effect, there was an outburst of yelling and laughter. The party was on the way. Second bottles were available on payment, or more free beer.

The entertainment followed. Bub Fuller was the master of ceremonies, a role for which he was typecast. There was the five-piece hillbilly band led by Corporal Scarfe, a singer of cowboy songs and a yodeller, sketches satirizing Air Force life and finally a choral rendition by pilots of off-colour ditties which I'd written out and reproduced to ensure a modicum of unison among the loud if not melodious singers.

The party went on at full blast until midnight, well after the last corks had been popped and the last keg of beer drained, by which time none of the participants was feeling any pain. It had been a riotous blow-out, doing more in three hours to strengthen relations between officers and men than any amount of talking and raising morale to its highest possible level.

The miracle of the evening was that no one drowned, that everyone returned safely to billets including the pilots who had to navigate in jeeps and lorries over flooded roads and across a swollen river to reach the village. Stories were recounted the following day of some who almost didn't make it.

Two days later, on October 22nd, the Wing was transferred out of waterlogged B.82 back to Brussels, first to B.58 Melsbroek and then on November 4th, to B.56 Evere on the eastern outskirts of the city. Although some distance from the front line we were reminded of the enemy from time to time by buzz bombs flying overhead en route to unknown targets. As there would be few operations until the weather cleared, I took a week's leave in London and on returning learned that the Squadron had logged in only two missions. For the time being the bashing of MT was over and we were back at altitude on patrols and on sweeps covering Bostons and Mitchells on bombing shows. There was a pause in the ground war as Allied armies prepared for the advance into Germany, and "softening up" of the enemy was part of the process.

Rewarded, someone said for good performance, 443 had been given the best of billets—a large, modern and well-furnished hunting lodge called "Chantleutje" in the country north-west of the base. It was owned by a wealthy Belgian family who had deeded it to the Air Force for the duration of the war complete with a non-resident caretaker who did the janitoring and whose wife did the laundry. Our little palace had a spacious living room with fireplace and record player, a large dining room, a well-equipped kitchen and seven sizeable bedrooms. With twenty-seven pilots the bedrooms were a bit snug even with double-decker bunks but compared to previous billets Chanleutje was heavenly accommodation, perfect for the maintenance of esprit de corps and ideal for parties. The first one, the house warming, was scheduled for November 6th.

I appointed a House Committee to maintain our new home in proper order and to establish rules of conduct for its inhabitants. These were posted in the entrance hallway and would have pleased the most exigent of mothers as they included injunctions on cleanliness, tidiness, care of furniture and equipment, social behaviour, and on aiming straight in the water closets. As to the party, I delegated responsibilities to five senior pilots for liquid refreshment, buffet food, decorations, record music and crowd control. To brighten up the affair we'd decided to invite ladies and I assumed the chore of searching them out, eventually finding twelve attractive CWACs living at the Atlanta Hotel whose supervisor agreed to release them into our care providing they were returned safely by midnight. My fellow C/Os offered their jeeps with drivers to pick them up at their billets and to collect them fifteen minutes before the witching hour.

The party was a great success. There was dancing, pilots sharing the ladies with exemplary good manners, singing in which the female choir competed with the male, tasty food and drinks of variety and quality. While Tank Sherman dropped a whole tray of champagne and Hodgins tried to ride a bicycle around the front room, no furniture was broken and no blacks committed. The CWACS entered fully into the spirit of the evening and added a degree of decorum to it though some of them had to be persuaded with gentle force to leave when the jeeps arrived to take them home. We all agreed that there was much to be said for the company of the fairer sex.

Weather was the enemy in November, putting up barriers of cloud, fog and rain and making patrols and bomber escort shows hazardous as well as unproductive. Typical of the latter was a raid on the marshalling yards at Oldenzall by forty-eight Mitchells and twenty-four Bostons, the Wingco leading 403 and 416 to cover the Mitchells and me following ten minutes later with 443 and 421 to rendezvous with the Bostons. Both were tricky do's because of cloud at several levels and heavy flak in the target area, and frustrating as none of the bombers could release their payloads.

A patrol of wry interest was one in which the Squadron was drawn into a dogfight with an aggressive bunch of American Thunderbolts who were determined to prove we were Messerschmitts and not Spitfires. We wondered later how many of us they'd claimed to have shot down. But you had to hand it to these American fighter pilots. While their aircraft identification was fallible they displayed great courage and bravado, peeling off in airshow manner and diving down, one after the other, into the deadly flak of the Rhur in search of ground targets and purple hearts. A near-tragic patrol occurred at the end of the month when engine failures forced Thomas to bail out of his burning kite, fortunately over friendly territory, and Wegg to crash-land in No Man's Land from which with good luck he escaped.

My two stalwarts, Smokey Stovel and Gordie Troke were now tour-expired and had been replaced as Flight Commanders by Bub Fuller and Phil "P.G." Blades. Bub was a rough-hewn bundle of good humour and enthusiasm and Phil had previously demonstrated his leadership ability as Flight Commander in 421. I was very happy to have this combination of skill and experience.

It was Phil and I who, on the 18th of November, discovered the Van der Aas, the Belgian family who were to become warm friends throughout the rest of the war and after. Driving by jeep, we were in search of beer for a second party with some of our CWACs and had been directed to a brewery in Velthem-Beisem, a village near Louvain. There we bought two kegs of high-quality beer from the owner, Mr. Van der Aa, brewer and mayor of Velthem, and were introduced to his charming wife, "Make," his pretty twenty-year-old daughter, Nelly, and his equally pretty niece, Dé. Phil and I fell in love with all three ladies and they adopted us as members of the family. Every Monday night we took three or four other pilots with us to their mansion-like home for dinners of unbelievable variety and tastiness served with wines and a large glass of milk for each milk-loving Canadian. These were followed by child-like tricks and games and some dancing with the two girls and the atmosphere of the evenings brought to all of us a refreshing kind of relaxation.

Although the weather continued to restrict flying, 443 had nearly as many shows in the first two weeks of December as in the whole month of November. On the 5th Johnnie Johnson led 443 and 421 on a sweep in the Munster-Rhein area but no Huns being reported on the return track the two squadrons separated, split into sections and scoured the roads for ground targets. 443's score included two riddled factories, one train badly dented, one gun position silenced, two horse-drawn guns stopped and three gasoline bowsers set on fire.

The first of several "Nickelling" raids started on December 8th. These were attacks on front-line German troops, not with guns but with disintegrating containers filled with leaflets which informed recipients they were doomed and invited them to surrender, showing the leaflet for safe conduct. The first distribution near Heinsburg was not particularly pleasant as our peace-making efforts received a hostile reception from enemy guns.

On the 10th, leading 443 and 403 on a sweep and armed recco east of Rheine, I spotted four Me 109s between two layers of cloud below and, ordering 403 to give cover, took 443 down after them. We got a few long-distance shots in before they scuttled into the cloud. In line with pre-mission briefing, we strafed everything in sight on roads back to the front line, the everything being no more than a few isolated MT and a troop of foot soldiers who broke ranks smartly on our approach. Two similar shows in the next few days were equally unproductive because of the persistent ground haze. There was considerable flak on the last one, however, Geldern and Ulmer being lucky to get safely home with large holes in their wings.

On December 16th three German armies under Von Rundstedt launched a counter offensive against the Americans in the Ardennes north of Luxembourg. As the weather limited air activity against them the Huns made rapid progress through the snow-covered hills and it was not until the end of the month and after heavy fighting that their advance was stopped.

443, now officially the "Hornet Squadron," was not engaged in supporting the Americans as on the 18th we were transferred for two weeks to No. 7 Armaments Training Camp at Warmwell in Dorset. The pilots were delighted to be able to spend the Christmas period in England and while I shared their feelings I was determined to give all of them, new pilots in particular, the maximum amount of training in air and ground firing before the battles ahead.

On Christmas Eve Phil Blades and I went to London to attend a dance at the Officers' Leave Club after which we spent the night on sofas in the apartment of two young ladies, respectable daughters of a minister of the cloth. Later there were some who doubted our story, at least about the sleeping on sofas.

My Christmas gift was a DFC. While secretly pleased about the decoration, I took it as no more than an award for seniority and durability. The boys were generous, however, and they celebrated with great gusto in the mess at Warmwell that night.

We'd heard about the massive surprise attacks by the Lutwaffe on aerodromes in Belgium and Holland on New Year's Day and when we returned to Evere on January 3rd we got the full story. The original objective of "Operation Herman," conceived by Goering, had been to give support to Von Rundstedt in the Ardennes by decimating Allied Air Forces but because of bad weather the attacks had been deferred to January 1st. The Germans calculated, in some cases correctly, that Allied pilots would not be very alert after the celebrations of New Year's Eve.

There were stories of heroism by pilots and ground crew during the attacks on B.56. Dave Harling, who'd become C/O of 416, took off while FW 190s were strafing the field, shot one down as he started to climb but was himself shot down before he could get sufficient speed to manoeuvre. Two 403 patrols that had been recalled to base shot down six Huns in the circuit. One airman had been killed and nine wounded, eleven Spitfires written off, twelve badly damaged and several transport aircraft destroyed. Post mortems of these bold attacks suggested that the toll would have been higher had the marksmanship of the Germans been better. From what we could see it had been pretty good.

One consequence of the fiasco for our Wing was the transfer of all aircrew from distant billets to the former German barracks on the aerodrome. We parted with tears from our luxurious hunting lodge and moved with groans into the concrete-walled buildings near the perimeter track that looked and felt like air-raid shelters. Four to six pilots were housed in each of the poorly ventilated rooms and I shared one with my two Flight Commanders, Fuller and Blades. Our pride and joy was an oil stove that provided a little warmth, lots of odour and clouds of smoke to add to the homeyness of our hovel.

We knew that 1945 would be the last year of the war and felt there were only a few months to go. "It's not the time to be faint hearted, the harder we fight the sooner it'll be over," I told the boys—and myself—over beer. But January started badly. On the 5th, Don Walz, leading a section of six, encountered heavy flak when strafing a factory and his Number 2, Gamey, went down in flames and Don was wounded and sent to hospital. After this show the Wing was grounded for a week by snow, sleet and fog, the only event being a tragic one when a disabled Fortress crashed and burned on the aerodrome, killing two of its crew as well as a 443 armourer attempting to deactivate one of the bombs.

Good luck came on the ensuing shows, most of them attacks on ground targets. On a squadron recco near St. Vith in the

American sector we destroyed or damaged thirty MT and on the same day, with six Spits of 443 and six of 416, we stopped a locomotive, damaged several freight cars as well as four army vehicles. On this show "Cookie" Cook of 416 was hit by flak but got home safely while Hal Fairfield, hit in the glycol tank, bailed out near Liege. There were two reccos on the 16th, one led by Phil Blades during which Tank Sherman's oxygen system failed and he, unconscious, spun in from 20,000 feet. It was the persistent yelling of his Number 2, Marsh that woke him up in time to pull out.

On a sweep with the Squadron on the 18th I spotted a twin-engine aircraft about to take off from the snow-covered west Rheine aerodrome and some black blotches that looked like planes at the end of the runway. With Marsh, my Number 2, to the right of me, I dived down, aiming at the twin, a Heinkel 111. Flak was plentiful but inaccurate as bullets from cannon and machine gun hit the twin squarely in the fuselage and sheered off a wing. The blotches further on turned out to be a snowplough, a dump truck and a gang of Jerries all of which Marsh and I made unserviceable. On the way back to base the Squadron put out of commission an important looking staff car and a flak wagon that was firing as it sped down a narrow road. When we returned I found that my "Ladykiller" had been the recipient of some of the fire, one of its wings punctured with little holes.

The Squadron had one last chance to persuade the enemy to surrender when Fuller, Blades and I led sections simultaneously on nickelling raids of German troops at Stralen, Geldern and Heinsberg. With heavy humour we added to the combat report: "Leaflet dropping missions carried out with great success and we expect immediate capitulation of enemy at all three places." More effective was an armed recco to the Malmedy area where we'd been called upon by the Americans to strafe Huns retreating from the Ardennes and succeeded in destroying and damaging more than twenty MT of various shapes and sizes.

The Wing was being re-equipped with Spitfire XVIs powered with Merlin engines built by the Packard Company in the United States. While this Mark was more powerful than the IX we were at times to regret having made the change as there were many engine failures. My new Ladykiller was a beauty but its engine was rough and it was only after my fitter had taken it apart that the fault was corrected. I was extremely fortunate in my maintenance team. Twenty-three-year-old Smitty, the fitter, looked like a teenager but had the touch of a magician with motors while solid and quiet-spoken Gordie, the rigger, tended the airframe as if it were his child. Both were fanatically proud of Ladykiller and worked without thought of time to keep her in shape. There were times when I felt I owed my life to them.

Brussels continued as the focal point for social activities, the Atlanta, Galla and Palace Hotels often replacing the mess as sites for thrashes, as well as for weekly hot baths. The most riotous thrash of the month, this one held for safety in the mess, was the farewell party for Group Captain "Iron Bill" McBrien, Station Commander of 127 Wing since the invasion and of the Kenley Wing earlier. Johnnie Johnson insisted that all pilots remain in the mess until the Groupie left, an order complied with to a man, drunk and sober. As his nickname implied McBrien was tough and authoritarian but he was always fair and everyone respected him.

He was replaced in the last week of January by Group Captain Stan Turner, DSO, DFC, who had served with distinction in both the Middle East and European theatres. Stan revealed his fighter pilot background and his grasp of operational problems at the first meeting he convened with the four C/Os. Among several of the measures he planned to introduce were the strengthening of administrative support for each squadron, the promotion of closer relations between pilots and ground crew and the reduction in the number of early returns to base by pilots reporting engine or instrument anomalies. In future fines would be imposed if it was shown that the pilot had failed to make an adequate cockpit check before departure.

The new Groupie shared my views about the need for flexibility in deciding when pilots should be tour-expired and he approved my recommendation that Bub Fuller, clearly on edge, should be retired and replaced by Don Walz, long overdue for promotion, and that Phil Blades should finish his second tour in mid-February. But you never told a pilot in advance of when he was going to be pulled off and I didn't tell Phil, keeping my fingers crossed that he wouldn't go for a burton in the interim. There had recently been a considerable turnover in pilots and so when reporting on the Group Captain's decision to a meeting of the Squadron I used the occasion to give the old pep talk to the newcomers. It always seemed to evoke a good response though to me it sounded like a scratchy old record.

There were fleeting signs of spring at the beginning of February, very fleeting we were to discover but enough to give us hopes of more action than in January, hopes that were in part realized. There were sweeps, armed reccos, escorts or "area cover" of bombers and in mid-February dive bomb attacks on railway lines. But German fighters seldom appeared and when they did they nearly always turned tail: aerial dogfights were things of the past and we were left mostly with the dirty and chancy work of beating up the Hun on the ground.

On the 3rd of February F/O Tegerdine of 403, taking off with his squadron on an escort job, had a miraculous escape when his engine cut out while he was still in the circuit. Going too slowly to turn, he glided toward a clear area, didn't make it and crashed on the roof of a four-storey apartment building. His wings sheared off, the fuselage skidded across the roof and came to a stop at the end, the engine balanced precariously on the parapet. He got out of the cockpit, walked downstairs and was taken to hospital for two stitches in his tongue. He wasn't as lucky a week later when he was forced to parachute from his burning Spit over Germany.

I considered myself a bit lucky on the 6th of February when leading 443 and 421 on an area cover of Fortresses bombing Berg-Gladbach. After the Forts dropped their bombs we escorted them back over friendly territory and then set course for base, flying between layers of cloud. To be sure of the course I checked with Kenway Control who, occupied with other Wings, passed me to Troytown Control on Channel A. Troytown gave a course of 310 and after twenty minutes informed us that we were over B.56. Letting down through the muck we came out over the Maas, fifty miles from base. I was a mite shaken as we were by now running short of petrol. Picking up landmarks through the haze I was able to get everyone safely down after a show of well over two hours. It wasn't too bad being lost when you were alone but when leading twenty-four trusting pilots it was not a pleasant experience.

One evening in the mess, Air Marshall Leckie, Canadian Chief of Air Staff, gave a talk on the war situation and answered questions on planning for the Japanese front after Germany had been defeated, being impressed by the large number of pilots who said they'd volunteer for service in the Far East. He went on to report that the RCAF was currently over-supplied with fighter pilots who had not yet had a chance to fight and were eager to do so.

Hearing this, I was more than ever determined to retire those in the Squadron who were at the end of their tours and had done their share. During February the Group Captain signed tour-expired forms for six of my veterans.

When Johnnie Johnson returned from a spell of leave, the Group Captain convened a meeting of all pilots in the Wing, the theme being the need to prepare for the big push in March. After giving a broad picture of war strategy and of the Wing's role in it, he concluded by emphasizing that good ground and air discipline and utmost keenness were essential. He then held a second meeting with the Wing Commander, C/Os and Flight Commanders to deal with specifics including take-off and landing procedures and efficient aircraft maintenance. Finally there was a third meeting with the Wingco and C/Os to discuss the promotion of esprit de corps. Clearly the Groupie was determined to put the Wing in first-class shape for the invasion of Germany.

On the 14th of February, Valentine's Day, the Squadron carried out three successful "railway interdictions." These legalistically-entitled operations were dive bombing attacks on railway lines designed to paralyze enemy movement by train. Carrying 500-pound bombs we dived like Stukas from 10,000 to 3,000 feet and released our bombs when pulling out, accurate flying and no diversion for flak being called for. On the first show I selected a railway line at Heldern and though the cloud was at 9,000 feet we got in four direct hits and nine near misses, near enough to weaken the roadbed. The second, on a line between Wesel and Dorsten was equally effective while during the third, on a marshalling yard and junction at Rees, all of my section of six dropped their bombs squarely on the targets. The total score for the day was thirteen direct hits and fifteen near misses, a creditable performance for Spits acting as Typhoons.

On the 18th I informed Phil Blades he was tour-expired. He protested, as expected, but I knew he was tired: he was eating nothing and in the air taking unnecessary risks. We went to the Van der Aas for dinner that night and there he was overwhelmed with gifts offered with affection from all the family. The next night there was a thrash in the mess for which he supplied the drinks and during which he sneaked off to bed to prevent any speechifying. Lloyd Hunt, his 2 I.C., replaced him as Flight Commander.

The weather improved on the 21st and the Squadron got in two armed reccos to the Wesel-Dorsten area where, breaking into sections and attacking in singles, we destroyed eleven MT and damaged thirty. There had been some flak but having successfully confused the gunners all the boys returned to base highly satisfied.

On the 22nd, with clapped-out Spit IXs, Peewee Dalton and I escorted a Dakota carrying the Speaker of the House of Commons to England. The return of the Dak was delayed because of weather and when we got back on the 24th there was bad news. Don Walz, leading the Squadron on an armed recco the day before, had been hit by flak, bailed out and taken prisoner. This was the second time Don had gone down in enemy territory, the first in France when he'd escaped with the help of the Resistance. This time he was lost for the duration and it was a sad blow for him as well as the Squadron. The Wingco accepted my recommendation of Chuck Charlesworth to replace him as O/C of the Flight. Chuck was an intrepid, slow-speaking Gary Cooper type with an English accent who'd had a good first tour in North Africa.

The Group Captain asked me to represent him at a farewell dinner on the 25th for General Montgomery at AOC Headquarters in Eindhoven. I got airborne at five-thirty and was the first to arrive at the mess in the Phillips country palace of champagne memory, feeling out of place until a friendly Air Commodore offered a beer. The affair started with hot rums and countless delicacies served by pretty waitresses, and a scrumptious dinner with speeches followed. Before the dinner and primed with rum I was holding forth on one of my favourite subjects—awarding decorations solely on the basis of scores and ignoring the courage and leadership of many others who were not good marksmen—when Broadhurst, the AOC, approached. "You're absolutely right, Sager," he said. I sobered up, surprised not by his agreement but by his knowing my name. Then I remembered everyone was wearing a name tag!

We were having serious trouble with the Packard-Merlin engines in our new Spit XVI's: internal explosions with connecting rods going clear through the cylinder. Three pilots had crashlanded and on the 24th and 25th two pilots bailed out over enemy territory. The engineers suspected either poor material or sabotage in American factories. To avoid further losses and restore pilots' confidence in their kites the Wing was grounded for two days for engine inspections and overhauls.

In this non-flying period Flight Commanders organized softball games while I got caught up on a multitude of administrative chores including the giving of gentle admonitions to three airmen charged with being AWOL, making out more severe reports on two pilots for foolish taxiing accidents, and writing to Don Walz's parents assuring them that he had landed safely in Germany. Other letters to the families of pilots shot down had been more difficult to write. And finally, when most of our aircraft had been test-flown I sent the new pilots up on familiarization flights. Watching their landings from Flying Control made me lose some of my youth as they were rusty from lack of practice.

American and British advances were going well, some of their forces being within shelling distance of Cologne and Dusseldorf. Everyone in the Wing felt frustrated as we could do little to help, low cloud and thick haze blurring out the rapidly-changing front line. Two armed reccos had to be aborted when we could not distinguish friend from foe.

The second of March was the day of the Wing's move to its new base, B.90, at Petit-Brogel in north-east Belgium near the Dutch border. It was also a busy day for the Squadron with two railway interdictions, the first between Emmerich and Wesel, the second near Borken. In spite of haze and flak we scored one hit and many near misses, our bombs damaging the roadbed in several sections. After the second show we landed with the Wing at B.90, the noise of our touchdowns on the steel-matted runway reminding us of B.2 in Normandy.

But there was a world of difference between B.90 and B.2. Our new base was brand new and we its first occupants. It had an excellent layout for services and maintenance, well placed and spacious dispersals and comfortable billets for all ranks in semi-permanent buildings of Nissen-type design. When the lorries with supplies, equipment and personal belongings arrived we settled in quickly, A and B Flights in separate units, the Adjutant and me, the two Flight Commanders with their 2 I.C. sharing a third. These two—Tank Sherman and Hal Fairfield—displayed great energy and ingenuity in installing extra lights, a second stove, a radio and other amenities. A quick reconnaissance revealed that fresh eggs were readily available from a nearby farm, though Tank quipped, "What's the use of an aphrodisiac in this deserted neck of the woods?"

Johnnie Johnson, enthusiastic about trying to catch Hun fighters now reported by Control to be showing themselves, led 416 and 421 on an early morning sweep but none appeared and he returned disappointed. I took 443 and 403 on a repeat perform-ance and got the same result. Returning over the west Rheine aerodrome we saw blotches that looked like aircraft lined up prominently along a perimeter track. Something told me they were dummies and that it was a flak trap and, squeamishly, I decid-ed not to have a go. My conscience was relieved later when Intelligence reported that my suspicions had been confirmed by a Typhoon Wing that had dive-bombed the dummies, fortunately without loss. Four other sweeps in the first week of March were all uneventful as, contrary to Intelligence reports, Hun fighters were still hibernating and the German army seemed to be travel-ling only at night.

At a meeting with the Wingco and C/Os on the 5th the Groupie announced that TAF had ordered a reduction in the number of operations for the time being, principally because of a shortage of Spitfires. Expecting an earlier end to the war, the Government had closed down some aircraft factories and con-verted others to the manufacture of war equipment in short sup-ply. To conserve our present complement of planes there would be no more bombing or strafing of ground targets until further notice and each squadron would be limited to no more than one mission per day. Squadrons were placed on a 24-hour shift system though pilots not on shift were required to report to dispersals at nine every morning.

Johnnie Johnson went on leave and during his absence I was made Acting Wing Commander, a post with few responsibilities when the Wing was on limited operations. I asked the other C/Os or their Flight Commanders to organize softball games and one day with Mitchener, C/O of 416, led a large gang of pilots on a two-mile jog to the nearest pub. I also started planning a Wing concert, a revue, using as the nucleus Corporal Scarfe's hillbilly band and singers who'd displayed their talents at the Squadron party at Grave in November. The objective was twofold: to occupy the spare time of the ground crew and to bolster morale in the whole outfit.

During this period of restricted flying many pilots drove across the line into Germany to sightsee and scrounge for whatever they could find, including cars. Tank Sherman returned with a smart little Mercedes-Benz and Hal Fairfield with an Opel convertible, both bought for next to nothing from impoverished inhabitants of Gladbach. Other items picked up included guns, cameras and radios. I'd no desire to participate in this activity having developed great sympathy for civilians of whatever nationality suffering from the devastation of war. The pilots recounted their impressions, particularly the tangible hostility of silent Germans, their eyes on the ground as they searched for food in the rubble.

When the Wingco returned, I had a heavy cold and took the jeep and drove to Velthem for a 48-hour break with the Van der Aas. There I was put to bed with aspirins and hot rum. Nelly woke me up the next morning for breakfast in bed, and I spent a day and night doing family things and forgetting the war.

On the 11th of March I led 443 and 421 on a sweep around Osnabruch and Guterslohn, flying below and above cloud, encountering some flak but no Huns and sadly losing a 421 pilot who had to bail out over Germany when his engine failed. A Wing escort of Mitchells and Invaders on the 13th was a complete shambles when the bombers got separated between layers of cloud, dropped their bombs haphazardly and forced the Wing to split up to shepherd groups of them back across the line. The 13th was also my unlucky day as I lost my beautiful

Ladykiller. I'd asked another pilot to test-fly it after an overhaul and he pranged it on the runway, damaging it beyond repair at the base. Two days later I got a new one, a smooth-running kite, and so few tears were shed.

Heavy bombers, Lancs and Forts, started bombing a wide area around Osnabruch and Munster, revealing the forthcoming drive by Allied ground forces. The Wing's task was to keep the skies clear of Hun fighters so the bombers could do their job unmolested. We succeeded but only by our presence as no Hun fighters intervened.

A dance was held in the mess on March 17th to which Canadian nurses from hospitals in the area had been invited. After it was over I took Tank Sherman's Mercedes and with Bob Hazel drove three of the girls back to their hospital in Zelst. Half a mile from the hospital on the return trip, speeding with dimmed lights along a shortcut, I did not see that the bridge across a dyke was no longer there; it had recently been bombed. At sixty miles an hour the car soared into the air and plunged into the water. With the malleability of the inebriated we extricated ourselves, swam to shore and hiked back to the hospital where, after a hot shower, we slept the night in one of the wards. Hal Fairfield collected us in the jeep the following morning and the Mercedes was later hauled out, towed to the base and repaired. I didn't submit an accident report.

This hushed-up black left me unprepared for two compliments that came my way a couple of days later. The first was from the Group Captain. He said he'd been studying the aircraft maintenance statistics and had found that 443's serviceability record during the past months had been the best in the Wing. He agreed I might pass his congratulations on to the N.C.O.s, which I promptly did, and they were as proud and pleased as I was. The second came from the Wing Commander over beer in the mess. He said nice things about the spirit of the Squadron and its performance, particularly on ground attacks, adding that 443 had been lucky in having had only two Commanding Officers on operations, a marksman and individualist, and a team leader. I could not have received higher praise.

On March 18th I had another encounter with suspected dummies, again on the West Rheine aerodrome. Passing over the field after a sweep with the Squadron, I saw what appeared to be FW190s lined up at one end of a runway. We circled but they didn't budge and there was no movement anywhere on the base. Remembering the flak trap of two weeks earlier I decided not to take the bait, regretting it later as in spite of the no-strafing rule I could at least have had a nibble. Guiltily I wondered if at last I had got the "twitch."

Losses of pilots and aircraft from engine failures had become our most serious problem. On the 9th a pilot of 416 had crash-landed in enemy territory, on the 10th a 421 pilot had killed himself trying to get his damaged plane down, on the 14th Messum's kite blew up in the circuit though he managed to get in with wheels down, on the 17th Weber crash-landed on the base, wounding himself badly, and on the same day Saintsbury made a dead-stick landing at B.80. Since the troubles began there had been thirty-four engine failures. On March 20th the Wing was grounded for modification of all engines and conversion to 18-pounds boost and 100 octane fuel.

There being no flying on the 21st, we organized a softball game with 421, 443 winning hands down. But the day was marred by two accidents of bomber aircraft on the base. A Mitchell, hit by flak and flown by its only unwounded crew member, a gunner, crash landed on the runway and in the afternoon two Invaders collided above the field and both spun in, killing all the crew except a bombardier who'd bailed out at low level.

The timing, on March 22nd, of the concert, a revue entitled "Hash and Ham," could not have been better. The Wing was inoperative and in the following week the push into Germany would begin. Most of my spare time over three weeks had been taken up in its preparation—the screening of performers, writing of songs and skits, rehearsing, constructing a stage and printing of programs. Sergeant Scarfe and his orchestra provided the glue that held all together as well as the accompaniment for the singing of the Six Joes and a Guitar, the Pair with Bullbass, the Old Timer's Group and the choral rendition of "You'll Get Used To It," the popular Canadian Navy song to which I'd set words satirizing aspects of life on the wing. There was also a hillbilly skit, a radio interview mocking wing personalities and two other comic numbers, one performed in German uniform. The bringing of all these items together and welding them into a unified, slick-moving show had not been easy and I was relieved when the curtain came down and happy that it did so to thunderous applause.

On the evening of the 23rd the Wing was briefed by the Group Captain, Wing Commander and Intelligence and Met Officers. March 24th was "R" Day, the beginning of the operation called "Varsity," the crossing of the Rhine. There would be massive airborne landings of paratroopers and soldiers in gliders to secure four major crossings. Pilots would be aroused at 4 a.m. for take-off at dawn, 443 being the third squadron off to patrol a line from Dorsten to Borken. After the briefing I gave a short pep talk to the Squadron; spirits were high and I went to bed proud of my team and confident about its performance.

"R" Day was a complete success for Allied armies but it was an anti-climax for 127 Wing. We were in the air continuously from dawn to dusk but not a single German fighter rose to do battle. The airborne landings were spectacular, the sky congested with aircraft towing gliders and parachutes falling like white blossoms. Smoke from earlier bombing formed a bank of thick cloud from south to north. I flew for seven hours, leading the Squadron on four operations. They may have frightened off some 109s and they also gave us a bird's eye view of the invasion of the Fatherland.

On the last patrol of the day Chuck Charlesworth's engine failed as he entered the circuit. Having no time to alter course, he crash-landed, coming to a stop with engine and cockpit only on the top of an aircraft bay. When ground crew rushed up to help him he waved them away, climbed down and then passed out. He was taken to hospital with concussion and a deep cut on the forehead.

Johnnie Johnson was taken off operations that evening and promoted to Group Captain of 125 Wing at Eindhoven. There was a thrash for him in the mess and before leaving the next morning he toured the airfield to say goodbye to pilots and ground crew. Wing Commander Johnnie Johnson, DSO, DFC, the fighter pilot with the highest score in the Air Force, left operational flying after a distinguished career, notably as the leader of Canadian Wings.

On the 25th of March I led the Squadron on two patrols, the first uneventful, the second ending up in a chase after two jets, surprisingly accompanied by two 109s. They were apparently after Fortresses above the cloud but on our approach they turned on their backs and went straight down, disappearing in the smoke and haze below. There were three patrols on the 26th and on the second, no Huns being seen or reported, we dropped down to 5,000 feet to look for MT, the no-strafing restriction having been lifted. Through the haze east of the front line we spotted a congestion of traffic on a small road and though there was a fair amount of flak we split up and attacked, destroying and damaging seventeen vehicles.

On an armed recco with 500-pound bombs on the 28th we got below 10/10ths cloud over Munster and dropped all of our payload squarely on a railway marshalling yard. Regaining altitude, I spotted four Me 109s above, just below the cloud. Throttles through the gate, we went after them. I got a long burst in on the nearest one, saw what I thought were strikes before he nipped into the white stuff but as he didn't come out all I could claim was another miss. Peewee Dalton, leading the section on my right, got strikes on another that were clearly visible and he was rightfully credited with a damaged.

The next morning, March 29th, I went to see the Group Captain to get his permission to take Lloyd Hunt off operations and replace him with Terry Watt, a former instructor and a very experienced pilot.

"Okay, Art, make out the form for Hunt," Stan Turner said, smiling. Then, as I turned to leave, he added casually, "I'm taking you off too, Art. As of now. It's time you packed it in." I started to protest but he went on.

"It's six months to the day since you took over the Squadron, you've put in well over two hundred hours and you've had a very good go. Tom de Courcy will take over 443 tomorrow and he should be allowed to choose a replacement for Hunt, a temporary replacement for Charlesworth as well as the new 2 I.C.s. Besides, we're moving to a new base in two days and there may be other changes. Congratulations, Art, you've done a splendid job!" He shook my hand but I couldn't say anything. I was stunned as I'd thought I'd be staying on to the end.

Going back to the dispersal it hit me that I'd be leaving the Squadron at a crucial time and almost went back to ask Stan to change his mind. Then, suddenly, I realized I'd reached the end of the line. Having read the signs of fatigue in many others I knew I was suffering from it: my nerves were taut, the turmoil inside bottled up. There was a little thrash in the mess that night, emotionally draining for me, and the next morning at eight one of the boys drove Lloyd Hunt and me to Eindhoven to catch a Dakota for Northholt.

It was while walking the streets of London that the reaction set in. I went into a blue funk of guilt and depression about deserting the Squadron and quitting before the war was over. Getting drunk in the Crackers Club didn't help and so, while waiting for a posting, I went for a week to my friends in Kent where, in their warm and affectionate company and after walking long hours every day, I finally recovered my balance and for the first time began to think about the future.

I boarded the S.S. *Ranchi* in Glasgow on May 2nd and when we were in mid-Atlantic Churchill announced the unconditional surrender of Germany. In Vancouver I was appointed Discharge Officer at the RCAF station at Jericho and when my papers came through discharged myself without worrying about the validity of it. I was in the reserve but Japan surrendered on August 14th and the long war was over. I felt I'd been lucky to survive it.

Painting by Ruske Rowal, presented by ground crew on leaving, April 1945.

EPILOGUE

After the war I became a rolling stone. Restless, beset by conflicting ambitions, I changed direction constantly, unsettling those dependent on me. One constant only—a persistent urge to work for a meaningful cause.

Thinking first of academia, I applied for postgraduate study at the University of British Columbia but the president, Dr. Norman (Larry) MacKenzie, persuaded me to postpone becoming a professor and to help him set up a public relations program for UBC. There followed two exciting years of creating an image of a likable Robin Hood who robbed other universities of their best professors and who stole army huts from everywhere to set them up on the campus as offices, lecture rooms and homes for war veterans and their families. All "vets" who qualified got in and enrolment tripled in three years.

This assignment completed, I was attracted to radio as an effective medium to inform the public on major issues and I accepted an offer from the head of the CBC, Western Division, to become Director of Talks and Public Affairs. Another two years of long hours and excitement, designing new programs and discovering hidden talent.

CBC headquarters in Toronto beckoned but Ottawa beckoned as well and I responded affirmatively to a proposal from the Federal Minister of Fisheries, Robert Mayhew, to become his private secretary. The two years with him were immensely satisfying, particularly when on missions abroad—to India for a United Nations conference, to Japan for discussions on fisheries, to Colombo, Ceylon, to participate in the Commonwealth Conference at which the Colombo Plan of aid to developing countries of the Commonwealth was established.

When Robert Mayhew became Ambassador to Japan I was offered the post of executive assistant to the chairman of the

Fisheries Association, the organization representing the BC fishing industry. It was a challenging public relations post of wide scope, including the mounting of a successful campaign to save the salmon runs on major rivers of the province from destruction by the building of dams.

In 1955 I answered an appeal from my friend Larry MacKenzie to return to the campus at UBC to revamp the Alumni organization, participate in a fund-raising campaign for $10 million and, later, to become Director of International House.

I was sure I'd found my cause when I was asked to take over the management of the United Nations Training and Fellowship Centre on the campus, which had been set up for three years to design new methods of training civil servants from developing countries who had been sent to Canada on short-term United Nations or Commonwealth fellowships.

When the centre closed I was called to United Nations Headquarters in New York, first to manage technical assistance projects in India and Nepal. Certain that I had now arrived where I belonged, I volunteered for the post of chief of the Technical Assistance Unit of the UN Economic Commission for Africa at its headquarters in Addis Ababa, Ethiopia. Here I was responsible for the management of a range of regional projects in planning, statistics, banking, trade and resource development. I returned to New York in 1967 to become chief of the Section for Africa in BTAO, whose officers manage all UN projects by country on the continent.

In 1970 I accepted an offer from the Director-General of the United Nations Food and Agriculture Organization (FAO) in Rome to join his cabinet. Here I served for ten years in a number of capacities. While I regretted being far from the field, I had the satisfaction of knowing that my work contributed directly to the well-being of people in developing countries.

I retired in 1980.

KEY TO ABBREVIATIONS AND TECHNICAL TERMS

2 I.C.	Second in command
bogey	Unidentified aircraft, friend or foe until identified, hopefully in time
CFI	Chief Flying Instructor
cine-gun	Camera operating in conjunction with guns, helpful in confirming claims
C/O	Commanding Officer
contrail	White condensation trail of a high flying aircraft
DF Homings	Directional Finding Homings
dispersal	Pilots' waiting hut/club room when on readiness
EFTS	Elementary Flying Training School
erks	Ground crew, bless 'em!
F/L	Flight Lieutenant
F/O	Flying Officer
F/Sgt	Flight Sergeant
I/O	Intelligence Officer
ITS	Initial Training School
M.O.	Medical Officer
MT	Motorized Transport
O/C	Officer Commanding
OTU	Operations Training Unit
P/O	Pilot Officer
P.T.	physical training
recco	Reconnaissance operation searching for Huns or ground targets
R/T	radio transmitter
SFTS	Service Flying Training School
S/L	Squadron Leader
W/C	Wing Commander
W.C.	water closet, toilet
Wing Shows	Operations involving all squadrons of a wing

A PARTIAL GLOSSARY OF PILOTS' TERMS
Circa 1943

Bandits	enemy aircraft
Kite	one's aircraft
Press tits	Start engines
Don't panic chaps!	Chad, when boxed in by flak
We'll just about make it!	Chad again, in another dicey situation
Intrepid	Sticking your neck out
Shakey do	Rough go
Get off your knees!	Morning-after greeting
Like shit through a goose	Not wasting any time
Quit twisting my arm!	Sure, I'll have a drink!
Turfed	Kicked out
Cheesed off	Fed to the teeth
Get clued up!	Don't be a clot!
Get behind me Satan and push!	Affirmative, with emphasis
What's the form?	What's the plan?
Put up a black	Break the rules, being a clot
We'll go thataway	A Freddy Green briefing, pointing vaguely
Unserviceable	Spitfire, or pilot after a thrash
Thrash, bash	A party high in beer consumption
Shooting the shit	Reminiscing together with some fabrication
Going into the smoke	Going into London for unspecified purposes
Have a go!	Exhortation, in the air and on the ground
Shamoozle	Wild dogfight or just a ruddy mixup
I figure, I reckon	Chad, in preface to the real gen

Shit on the toast!	A Freddy Green expression with many uses
Finger in to the elbow	An absolutely stupid clot
Twitch, twitchy	Nervous or plain scared
Dragging his ass	Lagging behind, a straggler in formation
Cute little weapon	Variation on a theme of admiration
He bought it	Shot down, killed
Tough Titty!	Too bad!
Flies like a turkey!	Not well
Beating his gums	Yakking too much
Sharpen the old eye	One of Chad's toasts at the bar

Note: credit for most of the above goes to Wing Commander Chad Chadburn and Squadron Leader Freddy Green.

The Foggy, Foggy Dew

When I was a bachelor I lived all alone
And worked at the weaver's trade
The only, only thing I ever did wrong
Was to woo a fair young maid.
I wooed her in the wintertime
And in the summer too,
But the only, only thing I ever did wrong
Was to keep her from the foggy, foggy dew.
One night she came to my bedside
As I lay fast asleep
She laid her head upon the bed
And then began to weep.
She sighed, she cried, she damn near died,
And said, "What shall I do?"
So I hauled her into bed and covered up her head
Just to keep her from the foggy, foggy dew.
Now still a bachelor, I live with my son,
And we work at the weaver's trade,
And every single night as I gaze into his eyes
He reminds me of the fair young maid,
He reminds me of the wintertime,
And of the summer too,
Of the many, many times I held her in my arms
Just to keep her from the foggy, foggy dew.

Roger of Kildare

Mother, dear Mother, may I go to the fair?
May I go with young Roger, young Roger of Kildare?
He's very, very handsome and loves me for my sake,
Mother, dear Mother, may I go to the wake?
Yes, my darling daughter, you may go the fair,
You may go with young Roger, young Roger of Kildare,
But though he's very handsome and loves you for your sake,
Keep your legs together coming home from the wake!
So, my darling Nelly she went to the fair,
She went with young Roger, young Roger of Kildare
He stuffed her up with candy, stuffed her up with cake,
And stuffed her up an alley coming home from the wake.
Six months passed and nine months passed
And poor little Nelly dropped her load at last,
She fondled it and cherished it and loved it for its sake,
And called the little bastard young Roger of the Wake.
Beware, my village maidens, yes, beware!
Beware of young Roger, young Roger of Kildare,
For though he's very handsome and may love you for your sake
Keep your legs together coming home from the wake.